Taste of Home

COPYCAT
FAVORITES

TASTE OF HOME BOOKS • RDA ENTHUSIAST BRANDS, LLC • MILWAUKEE, WI

© 2023 RDA Enthusiast Brands, LLC.
1610 N. 2nd St., Suite 102, Milwaukee WI 53212-3906
All rights reserved. Taste of Home is a registered
trademark of RDA Enthusiast Brands, LLC.

Visit us at **tasteofhome.com** for other
Taste of Home books and products.

ISBN: 978-1-62145-995-8
Component Number: 116700121H

Chief Content Officer, Home & Garden:
Jeanne Sidner
Content Director: Mark Hagen
Creative Director: Raeann Thompson
Senior Editor: Christine Rukavena
Assistant Editor: Sammi DiVito
Senior Art Director: Courtney Lovetere
Designer: Carrie Peterson
Deputy Editor, Copy Desk: Dulcie Shoener

Cover Photography:
Photographer: Mark Derse
Set Stylist: Stacey Genaw
Food Stylist: Shannon Norris

Pictured on front cover:
Copycat Fried Chicken Sandwich, p. 49

Pictured on title page:
Herbed Onion Bagels, p. 16; California Chicken
Club Pizza, p. 79; Frozen Strawberry Daiquiris,
p. 85; Grilled Lamb with Mint-Pepper Jelly, p. 62;
Chicken Pesto Sandwiches, p. 47; Homemade
Smiley Fries, p. 93; Black Tie Chocolate Mousse
Cake, p. 101

Pictured on back cover:
Sour Cream & Cheddar Biscuits, p. 84;
Copycat Nothing Bundt Cake, p. 103;
Copycat Southwest Chicken Salad, p. 41

Printed in China

INSPIRED BY
DOLLYWOOD®, *CINNAMON BREAD*

DOLLYWOOD'S CINNAMON
BREAD COPYCAT, P. 24

TABLE OF CONTENTS

MORE WAYS TO CONNECT WITH US:
SHOPTASTEOFHOME.COM

ASIAGO TORTELLINI
ALFREDO WITH
GRILLED CHICKEN, P. 80

125 COPYCAT RECIPES THAT TRULY DELIVER!

Do you ever want to treat yourself to a drive-thru classic but don't feel like leaving the house? Have a craving for a restaurant favorite, but once you get the bill, you regret the expense? Keep your budget intact from the comfort of home by preparing your most-loved restaurant dishes yourself! Simply turn to this fabulous collection of mouthwatering favorites from fast-food hot spots, coffee shops and eateries that are popular from coast to coast.

With the recipes included here, it's a snap to re-create the main courses, appetizers and desserts you could previously enjoy only while out to eat. Inspired by Starbucks®, Cheesecake Factory®, Red Lobster®, Rib Shack®, Burger King®, Chipotle Mexican Grill®, P.F. Chang's®, Olive Garden® and other restaurants, these secret recipes satisfy your hunger as well as your wallet.

RE-CREATE THE TASTES YOU LOVE THE MOST!

Whipping up an impressive copycat surprise has never been easier, tastier or more affordable! Best of all, you can relish these bites from the comfort of your very own home.

Eye-Opening Breakfasts: Start the day without hitting a drive-thru. From bagels and waffles to smoothies and granola bars, these recipes promise to awaken you and your taste buds.

Coffee Shop Favorites: Need your daily latte fix? Spend your time and cash wisely by making coffee house specialties at home.

Best Appetizers Ever: From mozzarella sticks to pot stickers, these snacks are perfect for parties.

Specialty Soups, Salads & Sandwiches: Mix and match these craveworthy menu staples for a marvelous lunch or light dinner.

Copycat Entrees: Forget the take-out menu. Fried chicken dinners, juicy burgers and shrimp specialties are here to jazz up mealtime!

Popular Pizza & Pasta: Turn your kitchen into an Italian eatery with menu classics inspired by Little Caesars®, Romano's Macaroni Grill®, California Pizza Kitchen®, Noodles & Company®, Sbarro® and Olive Garden®.

Favorite Odds & Ends: Find recipes for cheesy crackers, salad dressing, French fries, steak sauce and other store-bought bites.

Double-Take Desserts: Satisfy your sweet tooth with an impressive duplicate of a restaurant fave.

Not only does every recipe include a complete set of nutrition facts, but each dish was tested and approved at the *Taste of Home* Test Kitchen.

COPYCAT
CHEESECAKE FACTORY
CHEESEBURGER
EGG ROLLS, P. 33

INSPIRED BY
CAFE DU MONDE®, *BEIGNETS*
NEW ORLEANS BEIGNETS, P. 14

EYE-OPENING BREAKFASTS

Wake up on the right side of the bed with these tasty,
classic morning copies that taste even better than the
original—and cost way less too!

BERRY SMOOTHIE BOWL

INSPIRED BY: JAMBA®, *SMOOTHIE BOWL*

I've always loved smoothies but sometimes I want to linger over breakfast instead of sipping it on the go. That's when I make this Jamba-inspired smoothie bowl.
—*Josh Carter, Birmingham, AL*

TAKES: 5 min. • **MAKES:** 2 servings

- 1 cup fat-free milk
- 1 cup frozen unsweetened strawberries
- ½ cup frozen unsweetened raspberries
- 3 Tbsp. sugar
- 1 cup ice cubes
  Optional: Sliced fresh strawberries, fresh raspberries, chia seeds, fresh pumpkin seeds, unsweetened shredded coconut and sliced almonds

Place the milk, berries and sugar in a blender; cover and process until smooth. Add ice cubes; cover and process until smooth. Divide mixture between 2 serving bowls. Add optional toppings as desired.

1½ cups: 155 cal., 0 fat (0 sat. fat), 2mg chol., 54mg sod., 35g carb. (30g sugars, 2g fiber), 5g pro.

HAVE IT YOUR WAY.

Store-bought or homemade granola would add crunch, while a dollop of peanut butter or honey and a sprinkle of cacao nibs would make your bowl taste just like dessert.

BLUEBERRY TURNOVERS

BLUEBERRY TURNOVERS

INSPIRED BY: PEPPERIDGE FARMS®, *BLUEBERRY TARTS*

Growing up, I loved to heat up a Pepperidge Farm blueberry turnover for an after-school treat. I decided I'd try my hand at making them for my kids. I think they're really close, and my kids love them.
—*Christine Hair, Tampa, FL*

PREP: 45 min. • **BAKE:** 15 min.
MAKES: 8 servings

- 2 cups fresh or frozen blueberries, divided
- 2 Tbsp. sugar
- 1 Tbsp. cornstarch
- 2 tsp. grated lemon zest
- 2 Tbsp. butter
- 1 pkg. (17.3 oz.) frozen puff pastry, thawed
- 1 large egg
- 1 Tbsp. water
- ½ cup confectioners' sugar
- 1 Tbsp. 2% milk

1. Preheat oven to 450°. In a large saucepan, combine ½ cup blueberries, sugar, cornstarch and lemon zest. Mash well with a fork. Bring the mixture to a boil over low heat; cook and stir until thickened, 1-2 minutes. Remove from the heat. Stir in butter and remaining 1½ cups blueberries.

2. Unfold puff pastry. On a lightly floured surface, roll out each pastry sheet into a 12-in. square. Cut each into 4 squares; spoon 3 Tbsp. filling into the center of each. Fold diagonally in half and press edges to seal. Place on an ungreased baking sheet. Beat egg and water; brush over pastry.

3. Bake for 12-15 minutes or until golden brown. Combine the confectioners' sugar and milk; drizzle over turnovers. Serve warm or at room temperature.

Note: If using frozen blueberries, use without thawing to avoid discoloring the batter.

1 turnover: 400 cal., 20g fat (6g sat. fat), 31mg chol., 235mg sod., 51g carb. (14g sugars, 5g fiber), 6g pro.

BUTTERMILK
PANCAKES

CHEWY HONEY GRANOLA BARS
INSPIRED BY: KIND®,
HONEY OAT BREAKFAST BARS

There's sweetness from the honey, chewiness from the raisins, hints of chocolate and cinnamon, and a bit of crunch in my homemade bars. To save a few for later, wrap individual bars and place in a sealed freezer container. Whenever you want a satisfying treat on short notice, just grab one and let it thaw.
—*Tasha Lehman, Williston, VT*

PREP: 10 min. • **BAKE:** 15 min. + cooling
MAKES: 20 servings

- 3 cups old-fashioned oats
- 2 cups unsweetened puffed wheat cereal
- 1 cup all-purpose flour
- ⅓ cup chopped walnuts
- ⅓ cup raisins
- ⅓ cup miniature semisweet chocolate chips
- 1 tsp. baking soda
- 1 tsp. ground cinnamon
- 1 cup honey
- ¼ cup butter, melted
- 1 tsp. vanilla extract

1. Preheat oven to 350°. In a large bowl, combine first 8 ingredients. In a small bowl, combine honey, butter and vanilla; pour over the oat mixture and mix well. (Mixture will be sticky.)
2. Press into a 13x9-in. baking pan coated with cooking spray. Bake until set and edges are lightly browned, 14-18 minutes. Cool on a wire rack. Cut into bars.
1 bar: 178 cal., 5g fat (2g sat. fat), 6mg chol., 81mg sod., 32g carb. (17g sugars, 2g fiber), 3g pro. **Diabetic exchanges:** 2 starch, ½ fat.

BUTTERMILK PANCAKES
INSPIRED BY: CRACKER BARREL®,
BUTTERMILK PANCAKES

You just can't beat a basic buttermilk pancake for a down-home country breakfast. Paired with sausage and fresh fruit, this pancake is just like the ones you get at Cracker Barrel.
—*Betty Abrey, Imperial, SK*

PREP: 10 min. • **COOK:** 5 min./batch
MAKES: 2½ dozen

- 4 cups all-purpose flour
- ¼ cup sugar
- 2 tsp. baking soda
- 2 tsp. salt
- 1½ tsp. baking powder›
- 4 large eggs, room temperature
- 4 cups buttermilk

1. In a large bowl, combine the flour, sugar, baking soda, salt and baking powder. In another bowl, whisk eggs and buttermilk until blended; stir into dry ingredients just until moistened.

2. Pour batter by ¼ cupfuls onto a lightly greased hot griddle; turn when bubbles form on top. Cook until second side is golden brown.
Freeze option: Freeze cooled buttermilk pancakes between layers of waxed paper in a freezer container. To use, place the pancakes on an ungreased baking sheet, cover with foil and reheat in a preheated 375° oven, 6-10 minutes. Or place a stack of 3 pancakes on a microwave-safe plate and microwave on high for 45-90 seconds or until heated through.
3 pancakes: 270 cal., 3g fat (1g sat. fat), 89mg chol., 913mg sod., 48g carb. (11g sugars, 1g fiber), 11g pro.
Pecan Apple Pancakes: To flour mixture, stir in 1¾ tsp. ground cinnamon, ¾ tsp. ground ginger, ¾ tsp. ground mace and ¾ tsp. ground cloves. To batter, fold in 2½ cups shredded peeled apples and ¾ cup chopped pecans.
Blueberry Pancakes: Fold in 1 cup fresh or frozen blueberries.
Banana Walnut Pancakes: Fold in 2 finely chopped ripe bananas and ⅔ cups finely chopped walnuts.

COPYCAT KRISPY
KREME DOUGHNUTS

COPYCAT KRISPY KREME DOUGHNUTS

INSPIRED BY: KRISPY KREME®, *DOUGHNUTS*

Glazed warm straight from the fryer, these sweet, heavenly orbs of fried dough have garnered a loyal cult following that has endured since the first location opened in 1937.

—*Lauren Habermehl, Pewaukee, WI*

PREP: 15 min. + rising
COOK: 5 min./batch
MAKES: 1 dozen

- 1   pkg. (¼ oz.) active dry yeast
- ¼   cup warm water (110° to 115°)
- 1   cup warm whole milk (110° to 115°)
- ¼   cup butter, softened
- ¼   cup sugar
- ½   tsp. salt
- 1   large egg, room temperature
- 3½ to 4 cups all-purpose flour
    Oil for deep-fat frying

GLAZE
- 2   cups confectioners' sugar
- ¼   cup whole milk
- 1   Tbsp. light corn syrup
- ½   tsp. vanilla extract
- ⅛   tsp. kosher salt

1. In a large bowl, dissolve yeast in warm water. Add milk, butter, sugar, salt, egg and 2 cups flour. Beat until smooth. Stir in enough flour to form a soft dough. Do not knead.
2. Place the dough in a greased bowl, turning once to grease the top. Cover the dough and let rise in a warm place until doubled, about 1 hour.
3. Punch the dough down. Turn onto a lightly floured surface; roll out to ½-in. thickness. Cut with a floured 2½-in. doughnut cutter; reroll scraps. Place 1 in. apart on greased baking sheets. Cover and let rise for 30-45 minutes or until doubled.
4. In an electric skillet or deep fryer, heat oil to 375°. Fry the doughnuts, a few at a time, until golden brown on both sides. Drain on paper towels.
5. For the glaze, whisk together all ingredients; dip the warm doughnuts in the mixture.

1 doughnut: 339 cal., 15g fat (2g sat. fat), 18mg chol., 98mg sod., 46g carb. (25g sugars, 1g fiber), 4g pro.

FRENCH TOAST STICKS

FRENCH TOAST STICKS

INSPIRED BY: BURGER KING®, *FRENCH TOAST STICKS*

Keep these French toast sticks in the freezer for an instant, filling breakfast. Their convenient size makes them ideal for a breakfast buffet.

—Taste of Home *Test Kitchen*

PREP: 20 min. + freezing • **BAKE:** 20 min.
MAKES: 1½ dozen

- 6   slices day-old Texas toast
- 4   large eggs
- 1   cup 2% milk
- 2   Tbsp. sugar
- 1   tsp. vanilla extract
- ¼ to ½ tsp. ground cinnamon
- 1   cup crushed cornflakes, optional
    Confectioners' sugar, optional
    Maple syrup

1. Cut each piece of bread into thirds; place in a single layer in an ungreased 13x9-in. dish. In a large bowl, whisk the eggs, milk, sugar, vanilla and cinnamon. Pour over the bread; soak for 2 minutes, turning once. If desired, coat bread with cornflake crumbs on all sides.
2. Place in a greased 15x10x1-in. baking pan. Freeze until firm, about 45 minutes. Transfer to an airtight freezer container and store in the freezer.

To use frozen French toast sticks: Place the desired number on a greased baking sheet. Bake at 425° for 8 minutes. Turn; bake for 10-12 minutes longer or until the sticks are golden brown. Sprinkle French toast sticks with confectioners' sugar if desired. Serve with syrup.

3 sticks: 183 cal., 6g fat (2g sat. fat), 145mg chol., 251mg sod., 24g carb. (8g sugars, 1g fiber), 8g pro.

CREAMY
STRAWBERRY
CREPES

CREAMY STRAWBERRY CREPES

INSPIRED BY: IHOP®,
STRAWBERRIES & CREAM CREPES

Wrap summer-ripe strawberries and creamy filling in these delicate crepes for an elegant brunch entree.
—*Kathy Kochiss, Huntington, CT*

PREP: 15 min. + chilling
COOK: 35 min. • **MAKES:** 7 servings

- 4 large eggs, room temperature
- 1 cup 2% milk
- 1 cup water
- 2 Tbsp. butter, melted
- 2 cups all-purpose flour
- ¼ tsp. salt

FILLING
- 1 pkg. (8 oz.) cream cheese, softened
- 1¼ cups confectioners' sugar
- 1 Tbsp. lemon juice
- 1 tsp. grated lemon zest
- ½ tsp. vanilla extract
- 4 cups fresh strawberries, sliced, divided
- 1 cup heavy whipping cream, whipped

1. In a large bowl, whisk the eggs, milk, water and butter. In another bowl, mix flour and salt; add to egg mixture and mix well. Refrigerate, covered, 1 hour.
2. Heat a lightly greased 8-in. nonstick skillet over medium heat. Stir batter. Fill a ¼-cup measure halfway with batter; pour into center of pan. Quickly lift and tilt pan to coat bottom evenly. Cook until top appears dry; turn crepe over and cook until bottom is cooked, 15-20 seconds longer. Remove to a wire rack. Repeat with remaining batter, greasing pan as needed. When cool, stack crepes between pieces of waxed paper or paper towels.
3. For filling, in a small bowl, beat cream cheese, confectioners' sugar, lemon juice and zest, and vanilla until smooth. Fold in 2 cups berries and whipped cream. Spoon about ⅓ cup filling down the center of each crepe; roll up. Garnish with remaining berries and, if desired, additional confectioners' sugar. Cover and refrigerate or freeze remaining crepes in an airtight container, unfilled, for another use.

2 crepes: 415 cal., 26g fat (16g sat. fat), 115mg chol., 163mg sod., 40g carb. (28g sugars, 2g fiber), 7g pro.

HOW-TO

Voila, Crepes!

1. Pour and swirl. Lift and tilt pan, swirling to evenly coat the bottom.
2. Cook crepes. Cook until the top appears dry; turn over and cook for 15-20 seconds longer.
3. Make filling. In a bowl, mix together the filling ingredients.
4. Assemble. Spoon about ⅓ cup filling down the center of each of the 14 crepes; roll up. Garnish and serve.

FREEZER BREAKFAST
SANDWICHES

MOM'S FRIED APPLES

INSPIRED BY: CRACKER BARREL®,
FRIED APPLES

Mom often made these rich, cinnamon-
sugar apples when I was growing up.
I swear the folks at Cracker Barrel
copied her recipe!
—*Margie Tappe, Prague, OK*

PREP: 15 min. • **COOK:** 30 min.
MAKES: 8 servings

- ½ cup butter, cubed
- 6 medium unpeeled tart
  red apples, sliced
- ¾ cup sugar, divided
- ¾ tsp. ground cinnamon
  Vanilla ice cream, optional

1. Melt the butter in a large cast-iron or
other ovenproof skillet. Add apples and
½ cup sugar; stir to mix well. Cover and
cook over low heat 20 minutes or until
apples are tender, stirring frequently.
2. Add cinnamon and remaining sugar.
Cook and stir over medium-high heat,
5-10 minutes longer. If desired, serve
with ice cream.
1 serving: 235 cal., 12g fat (7g sat. fat),
31mg chol., 116mg sod., 35g carb. (31g
sugars, 3g fiber), 0 pro.

WHY YOU'LL LOVE IT ...

*"I thank whoever's mom made this!
It was fabulous. I made apple crisp
with the leftovers."*
—JACQUELINE BENSON, TASTEOFHOME.COM

FREEZER BREAKFAST
SANDWICHES

INSPIRED BY: MCDONALDS®, *EGG MCMUFFIN*

On a busy morning, these freezer
breakfast sandwiches save the day.
A hearty combo of eggs, Canadian
bacon and cheese will keep you fueled
through lunchtime and beyond.
—*Christine Rukavena, Milwaukee, WI*

PREP: 25 min. • **BAKE:** 15 min.
MAKES: 12 sandwiches

- 12 large eggs
- ⅔ cup 2% milk
- ½ tsp. salt
- ¼ tsp. pepper
SANDWICHES
- 12 English muffins, split
- 4 Tbsp. butter, softened
- 12 slices Colby-Monterey
  Jack cheese
- 12 slices Canadian bacon

1. Preheat oven to 325°. In a large bowl,
whisk eggs, milk, salt and pepper until
blended. Pour into a 13x9-in. baking pan
coated with cooking spray. Bake until set,
15-18 minutes. Cool on a wire rack.
2. Meanwhile, toast English muffins
(or bake at 325° until lightly browned,
12-15 minutes). Spread 1 tsp. butter
on each muffin bottom.
3. Cut the eggs into 12 portions. Layer
muffin bottoms with an egg portion, a
cheese slice (tearing cheese to fit) and
Canadian bacon. Replace muffin tops.
Wrap sandwiches in waxed paper and
then in foil; freeze in a freezer container.
To use frozen sandwiches: Remove foil.
Microwave a waxed paper-wrapped
sandwich at 50% power until thawed,
1-2 minutes. Turn the sandwich over;
microwave at 100% power until hot
and a thermometer reads at least
160°, 30-60 seconds. Let stand for
2 minutes before serving.
1 sandwich: 334 cal., 17g fat (9g sat. fat),
219mg chol., 759mg sod., 26g carb. (3g
sugars, 2g fiber), 19g pro.

NEW ORLEANS BEIGNETS

POWER BREAKFAST SANDWICH

INSPIRED BY: DUNKIN'®,
POWER BREAKFAST SANDWICH

When I'm looking for a quick breakfast on the go, I love to have these waiting in the freezer. I can grab one, pop it into the microwave and head out the door with something nutritious.
—*Jolene Martinelli, Fremont, NH*

PREP: 20 min. • **BAKE:** 15 min.
MAKES: 6 servings

- 1   tsp. olive oil
- ¼   cup chopped onion
- ¼   cup chopped sweet red or orange pepper
- ¼   cup chopped fresh baby spinach
- 6   large eggs
- ¼   tsp. salt
- ¼   tsp. pepper
- 6   Italian turkey sausage links, casings removed
- 1   pkg. (12 oz.) multigrain sandwich thins, split
- 6   slices cheddar, Swiss or pepper jack cheese

1. Preheat the oven to 350°. In a large nonstick skillet, heat oil over medium-high heat. Add onion and sweet pepper; cook and stir until tender, 3-4 minutes. Add the spinach; cook 1 minute longer. Remove from heat; let cool 5 minutes. In a large bowl, whisk eggs, salt, pepper and onion mixture. Divide egg mixture among 6 greased 4-in. muffin top tins. Bake until eggs are set, 12-15 minutes.
2. Meanwhile, shape sausage into six 5-in. patties. In the same skillet, cook the patties over medium heat until a thermometer reads 160°, 4-5 minutes on each side. Drain on paper towels if necessary. Layer sandwich bottoms with sausage patties, egg rounds and cheese; replace tops.
Freeze option: Wrap sandwiches in waxed paper and then in foil; freeze in a freezer container. To use, remove foil. Microwave a waxed paper-wrapped sandwich at 50% power until thawed, 1-2 minutes. Turn the sandwich over; microwave at 100% power until hot and a thermometer reads at least 165°, 30-60 seconds. Let stand 2 minutes before serving.
1 sandwich: 434 cal., 23g fat (9g sat. fat), 257mg chol., 1026mg sod., 31g carb. (3g sugars, 7g fiber), 30g pro.

NEW ORLEANS BEIGNETS

INSPIRED BY: CAFE DU MONDE®, *BEIGNETS*

These sweet French doughnuts are square instead of round and have no hole in the middle. They're a traditional part of breakfast in New Orleans.
—*Beth Dawson, Jackson, LA*

PREP: 25 min. + chilling
COOK: 5 min./batch • **MAKES:** 4 dozen

- 1   pkg. (¼ oz.) active dry yeast
- ¼   cup warm water (110° to 115°)
- 1   cup evaporated milk
- ½   cup canola oil
- ¼   cup sugar
- 1   large egg
- 4½ cups self-rising flour
     Oil for deep-fat frying
     Confectioners' sugar

1. In a large bowl, dissolve yeast in warm water. Add the milk, oil, sugar, egg and 2 cups flour. Beat until smooth. Stir in enough remaining flour to form a soft dough (the dough will be sticky). Do not knead. Cover and refrigerate overnight.
2. Punch down the dough. Turn onto a floured surface; roll into a 16x12-in. rectangle. Cut into 2-in. squares.
3. In a deep cast-iron or electric skillet, heat 1 in. oil to 375°. Fry the squares in batches until golden brown on both sides. Drain on paper towels. Roll the warm beignets in confectioners' sugar.
Note: As a substitute for each cup of the self-rising flour, place 1½ tsp. baking powder and ½ tsp. salt in a measuring cup. Add all-purpose flour to measure 1 cup.
1 beignet: 108 cal., 5g fat (1g sat. fat), 6mg chol., 146mg sod., 14g carb. (5g sugars, 0 fiber), 2g pro.

COPY THAT!

Rolling the beignets in confectioners' sugar can get messy. For a cleaner approach, place the beignets in a bag (paper or zip-top) with about ¼ cup powdered sugar, then close up the bag and shake lightly to coat. Working with a few beignets at a time—adding more powdered sugar if and when needed—is most efficient. Alternatively, you can sprinkle the sugar over top using a sifter or a sieve; this works well if you prefer a light dusting of sugar rather than a coating.

POWER BREAKFAST
SANDWICH

HOME FRIES
INSPIRED BY: BOB EVANS®,
GOLDEN BROWN HOME FRIES

When I was little, my dad and I would get up early on Sundays and make these for the family. The rest of the gang would be awakened by the tempting aroma.
—*Teresa Koide, Manchester, CT*

PREP: 25 min. • **COOK:** 15 min./batch.
MAKES: 8 servings

  1 lb. bacon, chopped
  8 medium potatoes (about 3 lbs.), peeled and cut into ½-in. pieces
  1 large onion, chopped
  1 tsp. salt
  ½ tsp. pepper

1. In a large skillet, cook the chopped bacon over medium-low heat until crisp. Remove bacon from pan with a slotted spoon; drain on paper towels. Remove bacon drippings from pan and reserve.
2. Working in batches, add ¼ cup bacon drippings, potatoes, onion, salt and pepper to pan; toss to coat. Cook and stir over medium-low heat until potatoes are golden brown and tender, 15-20 minutes, adding more drippings as needed. Stir in the cooked bacon; serve immediately.
1 cup: 349 cal., 21g fat (8g sat. fat), 33mg chol., 681mg sod., 31g carb. (3g sugars, 2g fiber), 10g pro.

WHY YOU'LL LOVE IT ...

"I cook breakfast for a men's group on Saturday mornings, and they wished I had doubled the recipe. It will be a repeat on a regular basis—fantastic."
—BONITO15, TASTEOFHOME.COM

**HERBED
ONION BAGELS**

HERBED ONION BAGELS
INSPIRED BY: EINSTEIN BROS.® BAGELS,
ONION BAGEL

I created my delightful bagels by combining elements from several recipes. I enjoy them spread with onion and chive cream cheese.
—*Pam Kaiser, Mansfield, MO*

PREP: 30 min. + chilling
BAKE: 15 min. • **MAKES:** 9 bagels

  ½ cup finely chopped sweet onion
  2 Tbsp. butter
  ¾ cup warm water (70° to 80°)
  ¼ cup sour cream
  3 Tbsp. sugar, divided
  3½ tsp. salt, divided
  1½ tsp. minced chives
  1½ tsp. dried basil
  1½ tsp. dried parsley flakes
  ¾ tsp. dried oregano
  ¾ tsp. dill weed
  ¾ tsp. dried minced garlic
  3 cups bread flour
  1 pkg. (¼ oz.) active dry yeast
  3 qt. water
  2 Tbsp. yellow cornmeal

1. In a large skillet, saute onion in butter until tender. In bread machine pan, place the water, sour cream, onion mixture, 2 Tbsp. sugar, 1½ tsp. salt, herbs, garlic, flour and yeast in the order suggested by manufacturer. Select the dough setting (check dough after 5 minutes of mixing; add 1-2 Tbsp. water or flour if needed).
2. When cycle is completed, turn dough onto a lightly floured surface. Shape into 9 balls. Push thumb through centers to form 1½-in. holes. Place on parchment-lined baking sheets. Cover and let rest for 30 minutes. Refrigerate overnight.
3. Let stand at room temperature for 30 minutes; flatten bagels slightly. In a non-aluminum Dutch oven, bring water to a boil with remaining sugar and salt. Drop bagels, 1 at a time, into water. Cook 30 seconds; turn and cook 30 seconds longer. Remove with a slotted spoon; drain well on paper towels.
4. Sprinkle 2 greased baking sheets with cornmeal; place bagels 2 in. apart on prepared pans. Bake at 425° until golden brown, 12-15 minutes. Remove to wire racks to cool.
1 bagel: 195 cal., 4g fat (2g sat. fat), 11mg chol., 415mg sod., 35g carb. (3g sugars, 2g fiber), 6g pro.

HAM & CHEDDAR OMELET
INSPIRED BY: PERKINS®,
HAM & VEGETABLE OMELET

This cheesy, full-of-flavor omelet is modeled after one I tasted and loved. Mine is so hearty and rich tasting that no one will guess it's lower in fat.
—*Bernice Morris, Marshfield, MO*

TAKES: 20 min. • **MAKES:** 2 servings

- 2 large eggs
- 4 large egg whites
- ¼ cup fat-free milk
- ⅛ tsp. salt
- ⅛ tsp. pepper
- ¼ cup cubed fully cooked ham
- 1 Tbsp. chopped onion
- 1 Tbsp. chopped green pepper
- ¼ cup shredded reduced-fat cheddar cheese

1. Whisk together first 5 ingredients.
2. Place a 10-in. skillet coated with cooking spray over medium heat. Pour in egg mixture. The mixture should set immediately at edges. As eggs set, push the cooked portions toward the center, letting uncooked eggs flow underneath. When eggs are thickened and no liquid egg remains, top 1 half with remaining ingredients. Fold omelet in half. Cut in half to serve.
½ omelet: 186 cal., 9g fat (4g sat. fat), 207mg chol., 648mg sod., 4g carb. (3g sugars, 0 fiber), 22g pro. **Diabetic exchanges:** 3 lean meat, 1 fat.

CHOCOLATE LOVER'S PANCAKES
INSPIRED BY: IHOP®,
CHOCOLATE CHOCOLATE CHIP PANCAKES

These indulgent chocolate pancakes are fluffy on the inside, with a rich but not-too-sweet cocoa flavor and a nice tang from the buttermilk. They are so delicious with maple or chocolate syrup—and even better with both swirled together on the plate!
—*Harland Johns, Leesburg, TX*

PREP: 15 min. • **COOK:** 5 min./batch
MAKES: 4 servings

- 1 cup all-purpose flour
- ¼ cup baking cocoa
- 2 Tbsp. sugar
- 1 tsp. baking powder
- ½ tsp. baking soda
- ½ tsp. salt
- 1 cup buttermilk
- 1 large egg, room temperature
- 2 Tbsp. butter, melted
- 1 tsp. vanilla extract
  Maple syrup and chocolate syrup

1. In a large bowl, whisk the flour, cocoa, sugar, baking powder, baking soda and salt. In another bowl, whisk buttermilk, egg, melted butter and the vanilla until blended. Add to dry ingredients, stirring just until moistened.
2. Place a greased large nonstick skillet over medium heat. In batches, pour the batter by ¼ cupfuls onto skillet; cook until bubbles on top begin to pop and bottoms are golden brown. Turn; cook until second side is golden brown. Serve with syrups.
2 pancakes: 271 cal., 8g fat (4g sat. fat), 64mg chol., 753mg sod., 42g carb. (16g sugars, 2g fiber), 8g pro.

LIGHT & FLUFFY WAFFLES
INSPIRED BY: WAFFLE HOUSE®,
REGULAR WAFFLES

These melt-in-your-mouth waffles are so tender that you can skip butter and syrup, but why would you want to?
—*James Schend, Pleasant Prairie, WI*

PREP: 15 min. + standing
COOK: 5 min./batch • **MAKES:** 12 waffles

- 2 large eggs
- 1½ cups all-purpose flour
- ½ cup cornstarch
- 1 tsp. baking powder
- ½ tsp. baking soda
- ½ tsp. salt
- ½ cup 2% milk
- 5 Tbsp. canola oil
- 2 tsp. vanilla extract
- 1 tsp. white vinegar
- 2 Tbsp. sugar
- ½ cup club soda, chilled
  Optional: Butter and maple syrup

1. Separate eggs. Place the egg whites in a clean, dry bowl; let stand at room temperature 30 minutes.
2. In another bowl, whisk together next 5 ingredients. In a small bowl, whisk egg yolks, milk, oil, vanilla and vinegar until blended. Beat egg whites until soft peaks form. Gradually add the sugar; continue beating until stiff peaks form.
3. Preheat waffle maker. Stir together the flour mixture, egg yolk mixture and club soda just until combined. Fold the egg whites into batter. Bake the waffles according to manufacturer's directions until golden brown. Serve with butter and maple syrup if desired.
2 waffles: 312 cal., 14g fat (2g sat. fat), 64mg chol., 421mg sod., 39g carb. (5g sugars, 1g fiber), 6g pro.

INSPIRED BY
STARBUCKS®,
PINK DRINK

PINK DRINK, P. 21

COFFEE SHOP FAVORITES

Start your day off right by skipping the dreaded early morning line at the cafe and enjoying your best-loved pick-me-ups from the comfort of your own kitchen.

MOCHA MORNING DRINK
INSPIRED BY: STARBUCKS®, *CAFFE MOCHA*

When I'm sipping this delicious coffee,
I feel like I'm visiting a coffeehouse.
—*Jill Rodriguez, Gonzales, LA*

TAKES: 15 min. • **MAKES:** 6 servings

- 6   cups hot brewed coffee
- ¾   cup half-and-half cream
- 6   Tbsp. chocolate syrup
- 7   tsp. sugar
- 6   cinnamon sticks (3 in.)
  Whipped cream in a can, optional

In a large saucepan, combine the coffee,
cream, chocolate syrup and sugar. Cook
and stir over medium heat until sugar is
dissolved and mixture is heated through.
Ladle coffee into 6 large mugs. Stir each
serving with a cinnamon stick. Garnish
with whipped cream if desired.

1 cup: 116 cal., 3g fat (2g sat. fat), 15mg
chol., 29mg sod., 19g carb. (16g sugars,
1g fiber), 2g pro. **Diabetic exchanges:**
½ starch, ½ milk.

COPYCAT STARBUCKS EGG BITES

COPYCAT STARBUCKS EGG BITES
INSPIRED BY: STARBUCKS®, *EGG BITES*

These are a quick, easy and delicious
breakfast . You can swap out the Swiss
cheese for Gruyere cheese and swap
the bacon for ham or add in small-cut
veggies. Serve with avocado slices
and fresh fruit for a healthy breakfast.
—*Maria Morelli, West Kelowna, BC*

PREP: 10 min. • **BAKE:** 25 min.
MAKES: 6 servings

- 6   large eggs
- ¼   cup 4% cottage cheese
- ¼   tsp. salt
- ¼   tsp. pepper
- ½   cup shredded Swiss cheese
- 3   cooked bacon strips, chopped

1. Arrange an oven rack at the lowest
rack setting; place a second rack in the
middle of oven. Place an oven-safe skillet
on bottom oven rack; preheat oven and
skillet to 300°. Meanwhile, in a small
saucepan, bring 2 cups water to a boil.
2. In a blender, puree first 4 ingredients
until smooth, about 20 seconds. Line
6 muffin cups with foil liners. Divide the
Swiss cheese and bacon among muffin
cups. Pour egg mixture over top.
3. Wearing oven mitts, place muffin
tin on top rack. Pull bottom rack out
6-8 in.; add boiling water to skillet.
(Work quickly and carefully, pouring
water away from you.) Carefully slide
bottom rack back into place; quickly
close door to trap steam in oven.
4. Bake 25-30 minutes or until the eggs
puff and are cooked to desired degree
of doneness. Serve immediately.

1 egg bite: 143 cal., 10g fat (4g sat. fat),
201mg chol., 311mg sod., 1g carb. (1g
sugars, 0 fiber), 12g pro.

COLD-BREW
COFFEE

COLD-BREW COFFEE
INSPIRED BY: STARBUCKS®, *ICED COFFEE*
Cold brewing reduces the acidity of coffee, which enhances its natural sweetness and complex flavors. Even those who take hot coffee with sugar and cream might find themselves sipping cold brew plain.
—Taste of Home *Test Kitchen*

PREP: 10 min. + chilling
MAKES: 8 servings

- 1 cup coarsely ground medium-roast coffee
- 1 cup hot water (205°)
- 6 to 7 cups cold water
  Optional: 2% milk or half-and-half cream

1. Place the coffee grounds in a clean glass container. Pour hot water over the grounds; let stand 10 minutes. Stir in cold water. Cover and refrigerate for 12-24 hours. (The longer the coffee sits, the stronger the flavor.)

2. Strain coffee through a fine-mesh sieve; discard grounds. Strain coffee again through a coffee filter; discard grounds. Serve over ice, with milk or cream if desired. Store in refrigerator for up to 2 weeks.
1 cup: 2 cal., 0 fat (0 sat. fat), 0 chol., 4mg sod., 0 carb. (0 sugars, 0 fiber), 0 pro.

DID YOU KNOW?

While many cold brew recipes don't use any hot water, we like the effect. The near-boiling water releases carbon dioxide in the grounds, extracting more flavor from the beans.

PINK DRINK
INSPIRED BY: STARBUCKS®, *PINK DRINK*
Whether you've seen it at the beach or on your favorite Instagram account, the Starbucks Pink Drink is still one of the most beautiful beverages we know of. Create your own version of the strawberry refresher at home.
—Taste of Home *Test Kitchen*

PREP: 15 min. + chilling.
COOK: 20 min. • **MAKES:** 2 servings

- 1 cup frozen unsweetened strawberries, thawed
- 2 berry-flavored green tea bags
- 1 cup boiling water
- 1½ cups coconut milk, chilled
- 2 Tbsp. simple syrup
- 2 cups ice cubes
- ¼ cup freeze-dried strawberries, slightly crushed

1. In a saucepan, cook strawberries over low heat until they start to break apart, about 15 minutes, stirring occasionally. Remove from the heat; cool. Using an immersion blender, puree strawberries. Chill, covered, until ready to serve.
2. Steep tea 5 minutes in boiling water; discard tea bags. Stir in the strawberry mixture, coconut milk and simple syrup. Divide the mixture between 2 glasses filled with ice cubes. Garnish drink with crushed strawberries.
1½ cups: 367 cal., 27g fat (27g sat. fat), 0 chol., 47mg sod., 28g carb. (23g sugars, 3g fiber), 4g pro.

COPYCAT STARBUCKS PUMPKIN BREAD

INSPIRED BY: STARBUCKS®, *PUMPKIN BREAD*

Skip the line and bake Starbucks pumpkin bread in your own kitchen. This copycat recipe might be better than the original!
—Taste of Home *Test Kitchen*

PREP: 25 min. • **BAKE:** 1 hour + cooling
MAKES: 2 loaves (16 slices each)

- 1   can (15 oz.) solid-pack pumpkin
- 4   large eggs
- ¾   cup canola oil
- ⅔   cup water
- 2   cups sugar
- 1   cup honey
- 1½ tsp. vanilla extract
- 3½ cups all-purpose flour
- 2   tsp. baking soda
- 1½ tsp. salt
- 1½ tsp. ground cinnamon
- 1   tsp. ground nutmeg
- ½   tsp. ground cloves
- ½   tsp. ground ginger
- ½   cup salted pumpkin seeds
      or pepitas

1. Preheat oven to 350°. In a large bowl, beat pumpkin, eggs, oil, water, sugar, honey and vanilla until well blended. In another bowl, whisk flour, baking soda, salt and spices; gradually beat into pumpkin mixture.
2. Transfer to 2 greased 9x5-in. loaf pans. Sprinkle tops with pumpkin seeds.
3. Bake until a toothpick inserted in the center comes out clean, 60-70 minutes. Cool in pan 10 minutes before removing to a wire rack to cool.
1 slice: 202 cal., 7g fat (1g sat. fat), 23mg chol., 205mg sod., 33g carb. (22g sugars, 1g fiber), 3g pro.

HAVE IT YOUR WAY.

Numerous mix-ins work well with pumpkin bread. We recommend adding chocolate chips or nuts and dried fruit.

YOGURT BERRY PARFAITS

YOGURT BERRY PARFAITS

INSPIRED BY: STARBUCKS®,
BERRY TRIO PARFAIT

Inspired by the Berry Trio Parfait at my local Starbucks, I layered homemade granola with fresh fruit and yogurt. It makes a superb breakfast.
—*Donna Speirs, Kennebunk, ME*

PREP: 30 min. • **BAKE:** 35 min. + cooling
MAKES: 8 servings

- 2   cups old-fashioned oats
- ½   cup pecan halves
- ½   cup sliced almonds
- ¼   cup sunflower kernels
- ½   cup packed brown sugar
- ½   tsp. salt
- ¼   cup butter, cubed
- ¼   cup honey
- ½   tsp. ground cinnamon
- 1   tsp. vanilla extract
- ½   cup dried cherries
- ½   cup dried blueberries

PARFAITS
- 2   cups fresh blueberries
- 2   cups fresh raspberries
- 2   cups chopped fresh strawberries
- 4   cups honey Greek yogurt

1. Preheat oven to 350°. In a large bowl, combine first 6 ingredients. In a small saucepan, mix the butter, honey and cinnamon. Cook over medium heat until blended, 3-4 minutes. Remove from heat; stir in vanilla. Pour over oat mixture; stir to coat.
2. Spread into a greased 15x10x1-in. baking pan evenly. Bake 35-40 minutes or until crisp and dark golden brown, stirring every 10 minutes. Cool on a wire rack completely. Stir in dried fruit.
3. In a small bowl, combine berries. Layer ¼ cup each berries, yogurt and granola in 8 parfait glasses. Repeat layers. Top with remaining berries.
1 parfait: 590 cal., 27g fat (11g sat. fat), 42mg chol., 294mg sod., 81g carb. (55g sugars, 9g fiber), 10g pro.

DOLLYWOOD'S CINNAMON BREAD COPYCAT

DOLLYWOOD'S CINNAMON BREAD COPYCAT

INSPIRED BY: DOLLYWOOD®, *CINNAMON BREAD*

Whenever I go to Dollywood, the first thing I do is run to the Grist Mill to get in line for the cinnamon bread. It's that good! I tried making it at home and think I got pretty close. I like using pumpkin pie spice instead of just cinnamon to give it a little more flavor.

—*Amanda Singleton, Kingsport, TN*

PREP: 30 min. + rising
BAKE: 30 min. + cooling
MAKES: 1 loaf (16 pieces)

- 1 pkg. (¼ oz.) active dry yeast
- 1¼ cups warm 2% milk (110° to 115°)
- 2½ cups bread flour
- ⅓ cup butter, melted
- 2 Tbsp. sugar
- 1 large egg, room temperature
- ¾ tsp. salt
- 2 to 2½ cups all-purpose flour

TOPPING
- ¼ cup sugar
- 2 tsp. pumpkin pie spice, apple pie spice or ground cinnamon
- ¼ cup butter, melted

1. In a large bowl, dissolve the yeast in warm milk. Add bread flour, butter, sugar, egg and salt. Beat on medium speed for 3 minutes. Stir in enough all-purpose flour to form a firm dough.

2. Turn onto a floured surface; knead until smooth and elastic, 6-8 minutes. Place in a greased bowl, turning once to grease the top. Cover and let rise in a warm place until doubled, about 1 hour.

3. In a pie plate, combine sugar and pie spice. Pour melted butter into another pie plate. Punch dough down. Turn onto a lightly floured surface. Shape into a loaf. Using a sharp knife, make 4 very deep slits straight across the bread dough (without cutting all the way through the loaf). Roll dough in butter, massaging butter onto all surfaces until dough is thoroughly coated. Roll dough in sugar mixture, firmly pressing mixture onto dough. Place the dough in a parchment-lined 9x5-in. loaf pan. Cover and let rise in a warm place until doubled, about 30 minutes. Meanwhile, preheat oven to 350°.

4. Bake for 30-40 minutes until golden brown. (Cover loosely with foil if top browns too quickly.) Cool 10 minutes before removing from pan to a wire rack. Serve warm.

1 piece: 215 cal., 7g fat (4g sat. fat), 27mg chol., 167mg sod., 34g carb. (6g sugars, 1g fiber), 5g pro.

Speedy Cinnamon Bread: If you don't feel like making your own dough, you can substitute a thawed 1-lb. frozen bread loaf. Cut the topping ingredients by ¼ and slightly decrease the bake time.

HOW-TO

Best Cinnamon Bread

1. Make a batter. The dough should be firm, not slack or sticky.

2. Knead. Turn the dough onto a floured surface. Knead until smooth and elastic.

3. Rise. Place dough in a greased bowl, turning once to grease the top. Cover and let rise until doubled.

4. Slash and season. Using a sharp knife, make 4 slits across bread dough. Roll in butter, then in sugar mixture.

CARAMEL FRAPPUCCINO
INSPIRED BY: STARBUCKS®,
CARAMEL FRAPPUCCINO

I love Frappuccinos from Starbucks, but they get too expensive. I now make my own, and they are just as good. If you blend the milk with the other ingredients, it gets too foamy—instead stir it in with a spoon after all the ice is crushed.
—*Heather Egger, Davenport, IA*

PREP: 10 min. + chilling • **MAKES:** 4 cups

- 2 Tbsp. ground dark coffee
- 1 cup water
- 3 Tbsp. sugar
- 2 Tbsp. caramel ice cream topping
- 2 cups ice cubes
- 1 cup fat-free milk
  Whipped cream, optional

Place ground coffee in the coffee filter of a drip coffeemaker. Add water; brew according to manufacturer's directions. Refrigerate coffee until cold. In a blender, combine the cold coffee, sugar, caramel topping and ice cubes; process until smooth. Add milk and pulse to combine. Pour the drink into glasses. If desired, top with whipped cream and additional caramel topping.
2 cups: 159 cal., 0 fat (0 sat. fat), 2mg chol., 122mg sod., 37g carb. (37g sugars, 0 fiber), 4g pro.

IRISH COFFEE
INSPIRED BY: BUENA VISTA CAFE®,
IRISH COFFEE

The Buena Vista Cafe in San Francisco claims to be the originator of Irish coffee in America. It serves millions of them a year, so who am I to argue! Since I can't get to San Francisco as often as I'd like, I had to make my own version. The Buena Vista doesn't add creme de menthe—that's my personal touch—but you can leave it out.
—*Marcia Whitney, Tampa, FL*

TAKES: 10 min. • **MAKES:** 2 servings

- 2 tsp. sugar
- 2 oz. Irish whiskey
- 2 cups hot strong brewed coffee
  (French or other dark roast)
- ¼ cup heavy whipping cream
- 1 tsp. creme de menthe, optional

Divide sugar and whiskey between 2 mugs; stir in coffee. In a small bowl, beat cream and, if desired, creme de menthe until thickened. Gently spoon onto tops of drinks, allowing cream to float. Serve immediately.
1 cup: 203 cal., 11g fat (7g sat. fat), 41mg chol., 21mg sod., 8g carb. (6g sugars, 0 fiber), 1g pro.

PUMPKIN LATTE
INSPIRED BY: STARBUCKS®,
PUMPKIN SPICE LATTE

Don't wait for your favorite coffee shop to bring back pumpkin lattes—make your own all year with this recipe. With just the right amount of spice, it tastes like the popular version everyone adores.
—Taste of Home *Test Kitchen*

TAKES: 15 min. • **MAKES:** 2 servings

- 2 cups whole milk
- 2 Tbsp. canned pumpkin
- 2 Tbsp. sugar
- 2 Tbsp. vanilla extract
- ½ tsp. pumpkin pie spice
- ½ cup hot brewed espresso
  Optional: Whipped cream, pumpkin pie spice and ground nutmeg

1. In a small saucepan, combine milk, pumpkin and sugar. Cook and stir over medium heat until steaming. Remove from the heat; stir in vanilla and the pie spice. Transfer to a blender; cover and process for 15 seconds or until foamy.
2. Pour into 2 mugs; add the espresso. Garnish with whipped cream and spices if desired.
1¼ cups: 234 cal., 8g fat (5g sat. fat), 33mg chol., 122mg sod., 26g carb. (24g sugars, 1g fiber), 8g pro.

INSPIRED BY
KFC®, CHILI LIME
FRIED CHICKEN

CHILI-LIME CHICKEN
WINGS, P. 34

BEST APPETIZERS EVER

These restaurant-inspired small plates, tasty bites and fabulous finger foods will have you forgetting to save room for the main meal.

HOMEMADE GUACAMOLE
INSPIRED BY: CHIPOTLE MEXICAN GRILL®,
GUACAMOLE

I always judge a Tex-Mex restaurant by its guacamole. It's simple to prepare but it can go wrong so easily. I've spent years perfecting mine, to the point where I think it's better than in most restaurants.
—*Joan Hallford, North Richland Hills, TX*

TAKES: 10 min. • **MAKES:** 2 cups

3   medium ripe avocados, peeled and cubed
1   garlic clove, minced
¼   to ½ tsp. salt
1   small onion, finely chopped
1   to 2 Tbsp. lime juice
1   Tbsp. minced fresh cilantro
2   medium tomatoes, seeded and chopped, optional
¼   cup mayonnaise, optional

Mash avocados with garlic and salt. Stir in remaining ingredients, adding tomatoes and mayonnaise if desired.
¼ cup: 90 cal., 8g fat (1g sat. fat), 0 chol., 78mg sod., 6g carb. (1g sugars, 4g fiber), 1g pro. **Diabetic exchanges:** 1½ fat.

HAVE IT YOUR WAY.
You can use lemon and lime juice interchangeably in this recipe to achieve a different citrus flavor. To substitute in orange juice, though, you will need to keep at least a little lemon or lime to spark up the taste.

HOULIHAN'S COPYCAT 'SHROOMS

HOULIHAN'S COPYCAT 'SHROOMS
INSPIRED BY: HOULIHAN'S®, *'SHROOMS*

I enjoyed this appetizer at Houlihan's restaurant and ordered it every time I went. When the restaurant closed in my area, I was determined to re-create the app at home. The mushrooms might even be better than at the restaurant! Besides just baking them, I have cooked them on a grill or in a toaster oven set on broil. They're enjoyed by everyone who has tried them.
—*Jo Hart, Flippin, AR*

PREP: 25 min. • **BAKE:** 15 min.
MAKES: about 1½ dozen

1   lb. small fresh portobello mushrooms
4   Tbsp. butter, divided
⅓   cup finely chopped onion
1   pkg. (8 oz.) cream cheese, cubed
½   tsp. seasoned salt
⅓   cup finely shredded cheddar cheese

TOPPING
¼   cup crushed Ritz crackers
1   Tbsp. butter, melted

1. Preheat oven to 375°. Remove stems from mushrooms and finely chop stems; set the caps aside. In a large skillet, melt 2 Tbsp. butter over medium heat. Add chopped stems and onion; cook and stir until tender, 4-6 minutes.
2. Add cream cheese and seasoned salt; cook and stir until cream cheese is melted. Fill mushroom caps. Melt remaining 2 Tbsp. butter. Dip bottoms of mushrooms into melted butter; place on a baking sheet. Top with the cheddar cheese. For topping, combine crackers and butter; sprinkle over tops.
3. Bake until mushrooms are tender and heated through, 12-15 minutes. Serve hot.
1 stuffed mushroom: 95 cal., 9g fat (5g sat. fat), 23mg chol., 131mg sod., 3g carb. (1g sugars, 0 fiber), 2g pro.

CAJUN FRIES WITH MALT VINEGAR SAUCE

CAJUN FRIES WITH MALT VINEGAR SAUCE
INSPIRED BY: FIVE GUYS®, *CAJUN FRIES*

Five Guys' fries have tons of devotees—and for good reason. My family is partial to the Cajun fries, specifically, which are super easy to make at home with your own seasoning blend. Air-fried instead of deep-fried, this salty, smoky, subtly sweet recipe is better for you than the original but just as tasty.
—*Julie Peterson, Crofton, MD*

TAKES: 30 min. • **MAKES:** 4 servings

- 1 lb. russet potatoes
- 1½ tsp. peanut oil

CAJUN SEASONING
- 1 tsp. sugar
- 1 tsp. smoked paprika
- ½ tsp. salt
- ½ tsp. garlic powder
- ½ tsp. onion powder
- ½ tsp. crushed red pepper flakes
- ½ tsp. dried oregano

DIPPING SAUCE
- ¼ cup mayonnaise
- ¼ cup ketchup
- 4½ tsp. malt vinegar

Preheat air fryer to 400°. Cut potatoes into ¼-in. julienned strips; toss with oil. Combine Cajun seasoning ingredients. Sprinkle over the potatoes; toss to coat. Place potatoes in greased air fryer. Cook until browned and crisp, 12-14 minutes, shaking once to redistribute. Combine dipping sauce ingredients; serve with the fries.

Note: In our testing, we find that cook times vary dramatically between brands of air fryers. As a result, we give wider than normal ranges on suggested cook times. Begin checking at the first time listed and adjust as needed.

1 serving: 216 cal., 12g fat (2g sat. fat), 5mg chol., 563mg sod., 26g carb. (6g sugars, 3g fiber), 3g pro.

Oven version: Prepare potatoes as directed. Place on a greased baking sheet. Bake at 450° until golden brown and crispy, 18-20 minutes, turning once. Serve with sauce.

MOZZARELLA STICKS
INSPIRED BY: OLIVE GARDEN®,
MOZZARELLA STICKS

While I always get mozzarella sticks when I'm at Olive Garden, sometimes I like to make them at home. My version is baked, not deep-fried, but if you want to hold true to the original, go ahead and drop them into some hot oil.
—*Mary Merchant, Barre, VT*

PREP: 15 min. + freezing
BAKE: 10 min. • **MAKES:** 6 servings

- 3 Tbsp. all-purpose flour
- 2 large eggs
- 1 Tbsp. water
- 1 cup dry bread crumbs
- 2½ tsp. Italian seasoning
- ½ tsp. garlic powder
- ⅛ tsp. pepper
- 12 sticks string cheese
  Cooking spray
- 1 cup marinara or spaghetti sauce, heated

1. Place flour in a shallow bowl. In another shallow bowl, beat eggs and water. In a third shallow bowl, combine the bread crumbs, Italian seasoning, garlic powder and pepper. Coat the cheese sticks with flour, then dip into egg mixture and coat with bread crumb mixture. Repeat egg and bread crumb coatings. Cover and freeze for at least 2 hours or overnight.
2. Place on a parchment-lined baking sheet; spray with cooking spray. Bake, uncovered, at 400° for 6-8 minutes or until heated through. Allow to stand for 3-5 minutes before serving. Serve with marinara or spaghetti sauce for dipping.
2 sticks: 312 cal., 17g fat (10g sat. fat), 116mg chol., 749mg sod., 22g carb. (4g sugars, 1g fiber), 20g pro.

SPICY SPINACH &
ARTICHOKE DIP

SPICY SPINACH & ARTICHOKE DIP

INSPIRED BY: CALIFORNIA PIZZA KITCHEN®, *HOT SPINACH DIP*

This is my take on California Pizza Kitchen's Hot Spinach Dip. I added artichoke hearts for extra flavor and texture plus chiles for a kick. I always use a flavored salt (in this case, celery) for more flavor.

—Michaela Rosenthal, Woodland Hills, CA

PREP: 20 min. • **BAKE:** 40 min.
MAKES: 3 cups

- 1 pkg. (8 oz.) cream cheese, softened
- ⅓ cup mayonnaise
- ¼ cup shredded Parmesan cheese
- ¼ cup shredded Asiago cheese
- 1 tsp. dried minced garlic
- 1 tsp. dried parsley flakes
- ½ tsp. celery salt
- 1 can (14 oz.) water-packed artichoke hearts, drained and coarsely chopped
- 5 oz. frozen chopped spinach, thawed and squeezed dry (about ½ cup)
- 1 can (4 oz.) chopped green chiles, drained
- 1 jar (2 oz.) diced pimientos, drained
- ⅓ cup shredded part-skim mozzarella cheese
  Tortilla chips or cubed sourdough bread

MINI MAC & CHEESE BITES

1. Preheat oven to 350°. In a large bowl, beat first 7 ingredients until combined. Stir in artichokes, spinach, chiles and pimientos. Transfer to a greased 3-cup baking dish; sprinkle with mozzarella. Place on a rimmed baking sheet.
2. Bake for 40-45 minutes or until hot and bubbly. Serve the dip with tortilla chips or bread.

¼ cup: 150 cal., 13g fat (6g sat. fat), 27mg chol., 324mg sod., 5g carb. (1g sugars, 1g fiber), 5g pro.

MINI MAC & CHEESE BITES

INSPIRED BY: OUTBACK STEAKHOUSE®, *MAC & CHEESE BITES*

Young relatives were coming over for a party, so I wanted something fun for them. To my surprise, it was the adults who devoured these mac bites.

—Kate Mainiero, Elizaville, NY

PREP: 35 min. • **BAKE:** 10 min.
MAKES: 3 dozen

- 2 cups uncooked elbow macaroni
- 1 cup seasoned bread crumbs, divided
- 2 Tbsp. butter
- 2 Tbsp. all-purpose flour
- ½ tsp. onion powder
- ½ tsp. garlic powder
- ½ tsp. seasoned salt
- 1¾ cups 2% milk
- 2 cups shredded sharp cheddar cheese, divided
- 1 cup shredded Swiss cheese
- ¾ cup biscuit/baking mix
- 2 large eggs, room temperature, lightly beaten

1. Preheat oven to 425°. Cook macaroni according to package directions; drain.
2. Meanwhile, sprinkle ¼ cup bread crumbs into 36 greased mini-muffin cups. In a large saucepan, melt butter over medium heat. Stir in flour and seasonings until smooth; gradually whisk in milk. Bring to a boil, stirring constantly; cook and stir until thickened, 1-2 minutes. Stir in 1 cup cheddar cheese and Swiss cheese until melted.
3. Remove from heat; stir in biscuit mix, eggs and ½ cup bread crumbs. Add the macaroni; toss to coat. Spoon about 2 Tbsp. macaroni mixture into each of the prepared mini-muffin cups; sprinkle with remaining cheddar cheese and bread crumbs.
4. Bake until golden brown, 8-10 minutes. Cool in pans 5 minutes before serving.

1 appetizer: 91 cal., 5g fat (3g sat. fat), 22mg chol., 162mg sod., 8g carb. (1g sugars, 0 fiber), 4g pro.

WHITE CHEESE DIP
INSPIRED BY: CHIPOTLE MEXICAN GRILL®,
QUESO BLANCO

Because my family loves the Queso Blanco from Chipotle, I wanted to re-create it at home! After many failed attempts, did I succeed? You be the judge! I've tried a generic brand of white American cheese singles, but it did not achieve the same creaminess as Kraft did. And the result is amazing!
—*Amy Enoch, Carthage, TN*

TAKES: 20 min. • **MAKES:** 3 cups

- 20 slices white American cheese, chopped (such as Kraft singles)
- 1 cup heavy whipping cream
- 6 Tbsp. salsa verde
- 3 Tbsp. juice from pickled jalapeno slices
- 3 Tbsp. pickled jalapeno slices, finely chopped
- 1½ tsp. reduced-sodium taco seasoning
   Tortilla chips

Combine all ingredients in a large microwave-safe bowl. Microwave, covered, for 6-7 minutes on high until mixture is smooth and heated through, stirring frequently. Serve warm with tortilla chips.
¼ cup : 139 cal., 14g fat (9g sat. fat), 45mg chol., 68mg sod., 2g carb. (1g sugars, 0 fiber), 1g pro.

CRISPY CRAB RANGOON

CRISPY CRAB RANGOON
INSPIRED BY: P.F. CHANG'S®,
HAND-FOLDED CRAB WONTONS

My husband loved the appetizers we had at P.F. Chang's so much, I was determined to make them at home. After several more trips to that eatery to taste them again, I had them perfected. I often prepare the filling earlier in the day to save time later.
—*Cathy Blankman, Warroad, MN*

TAKES: 30 min. • **MAKES:** 16 appetizers

- 3 oz. cream cheese, softened
- 2 green onions, finely chopped
- ¼ cup finely chopped imitation crabmeat
- 1 tsp. minced garlic
- 16 wonton wrappers
   Oil for frying
   Sweet-and-sour sauce

1. In a small bowl, beat cream cheese until smooth. Stir in the onions, crab and garlic.
2. Place about 1½ tsp. in the center of a wonton wrapper. (Keep remaining wrappers covered with a damp paper towel until ready to use.) Moisten edges with water; fold opposite corners over filling and press to seal. Repeat.
3. In an electric skillet, heat 1 in. oil to 375°. Fry wontons in batches until golden brown, about 1 minute on each side. Drain on paper towels. Serve with sweet-and-sour sauce.
1 rangoon: 61 cal., 4g fat (1g sat. fat), 6mg chol., 77mg sod., 5g carb. (0 sugars, 0 fiber), 1g pro.

COPY THAT!
To keep crab rangoons from exploding, try freezing the filled rangoons for about 15 minutes before placing them in the skillet. That way, they'll come out crispy and with no leakage. Also, when making the rangoons, be sure to fold the wonton wrappers in batches so the water won't dry out around the wrappers' edges. If the edges dry out, the rangoons will unfold.

COPYCAT CHEESECAKE FACTORY CHEESEBURGER EGG ROLLS

COPYCAT CHEESECAKE FACTORY CHEESEBURGER EGG ROLLS

INSPIRED BY: CHEESECAKE FACTORY®, *CHEESEBURGER EGG ROLLS*

Filled with ground beef, a smattering of crumbled bacon, diced pickles and plenty of melty cheddar cheese, these crunchy wonton-wrapped wonders are bestsellers for a reason. Now you can whip up a batch at home.

—Taste of Home *Test Kitchen*

PREP: 30 min. • **COOK:** 20 min.
MAKES: 1 dozen (1½ cups sauce)

- 1   lb. ground beef
- 1   small onion, chopped
- 2   garlic cloves, minced
- 1   cup shredded cheddar cheese
- ½   cup chopped dill pickles
- 4   bacon strips, cooked and crumbled
- 1   Tbsp. Worcestershire sauce
- 1   Tbsp. yellow mustard
- 1   Tbsp. ketchup
- ¼   tsp. salt
- ¼   tsp. pepper
- 14 egg roll wrappers
- 1   large egg, lightly beaten
     Oil for deep-fat frying

DIPPING SAUCE
- 1   cup mayonnaise
- ½   cup ketchup
- ½   tsp. garlic powder
- ½   tsp. paprika

1. In a large skillet, cook beef, onion and garlic over medium heat 4-5 minutes or until beef is no longer pink and onion is tender, breaking up beef into crumbles; drain. Return to pan. Stir in the cheese, pickles, bacon, Worcestershire sauce, mustard, ketchup, salt and pepper.
2. With 1 corner of an egg roll wrapper facing you, place about ⅓ cup filling just below the center of wrapper. (Cover remaining wrappers with a damp paper towel until ready to use.) Fold bottom corner over filling; moisten remaining wrapper edges with beaten egg. Fold side corners toward center over filling. Roll egg roll up tightly, pressing at tip to seal. Repeat.
3. In an electric skillet or deep-fat fryer, heat oil to 375°. Fry egg rolls, a few at a time, until golden brown, 3-4 minutes, turning occasionally. Drain on paper towels. Combine sauce ingredients; serve with egg rolls.
1 egg roll with 2 Tbsp. sauce: 451 cal., 32g fat (7g sat. fat), 61mg chol., 712mg sod., 26g carb. (4g sugars, 1g fiber), 14g pro.

HOW-TO

Preparing egg rolls is a snap with these tips:

- Drain the fat well from the cooked beef to keep the egg rolls crunchy.
- For successful folding and rolling, be sure not to overstuff the egg rolls with filling.
- Turn the egg rolls while frying so that they brown evenly on all sides.

CHILI-LIME CHICKEN WINGS

PORK & CHIVE POT STICKERS
INSPIRED BY: NOODLES & COMPANY®, *POTSTICKERS*

Here's my top make-ahead appetizer. The pot stickers are a lot more nutritious than the ones you get at a restaurant.
—*Marisa Raponi, Vaughan, ON*

PREP: 1 hour • **COOK:** 5 min./batch
MAKES: 5 dozen

- 2 medium carrots, finely chopped
- 1 small onion, finely chopped
- ½ cup finely chopped water chestnuts
- ⅓ cup minced fresh chives
- 1 large egg white, lightly beaten
- 3 Tbsp. reduced-sodium soy sauce
- ½ tsp. pepper
- 1 lb. ground pork
- 60 pot sticker or gyoza wrappers
- 3 Tbsp. canola oil, divided
- 1 cup chicken broth, divided

1. In a large bowl, combine the first 7 ingredients. Add pork; mix lightly but thoroughly. Place 1 scant Tbsp. filling in the center of each wrapper. (Cover remaining wrappers with a damp paper towel until ready to use.)
2. Moisten wrapper edges with water. Fold wrapper over filling; seal edges, pleating the front side several times to form a pleated pouch. Stand pot stickers on a work surface to flatten the bottoms; curve slightly to form crescent shapes if desired.
3. In a large nonstick skillet, heat 1 Tbsp. oil over medium-high heat. Arrange a third of the pot stickers in concentric circles in pan, flat side down; cook until bottoms are golden brown, 1-2 minutes.
4. Carefully add ⅓ cup broth (broth may splatter); reduce heat to medium-low. Cook, covered, until the broth is almost absorbed and filling is cooked through, 2-3 minutes. Uncover; cook until bottoms are crisp and the broth is completely evaporated, about 1 minute. Repeat with remaining oil, pot stickers and broth. If desired, serve with additional soy sauce and top with additional chives.
Note: If desired, wonton wrappers may be substituted for pot sticker or gyoza wrappers. Stack 2 or 3 wonton wrappers on a work surface; cut into circles with a 3½-in. biscuit or round cookie cutter. Fill and wrap as directed.
1 pot sticker: 39 cal., 2g fat (0 sat. fat), 6mg chol., 66mg sod., 4g carb. (0 sugars, 0 fiber), 2g pro.

CHILI-LIME CHICKEN WINGS
INSPIRED BY: KFC®, *CHILI LIME FRIED CHICKEN*

Who would have guessed that mixing maple syrup, chili sauce and lime juice would make chicken wings taste so good? Family and guests alike will scramble to ensure they get more than one of these utterly delicious wings—so be sure to make extras!
—*Taste of Home Test Kitchen*

PREP: 20 min. • **COOK:** 10 min./batch
MAKES: 2 dozen

- 2½ lbs. whole chicken wings
- 1 cup maple syrup
- ⅔ cup chili sauce
- 2 Tbsp. lime juice
- 2 Tbsp. Dijon mustard
- 1 cup all-purpose flour
- 2 tsp. salt
- 2 tsp. paprika
- ¼ tsp. pepper
  Oil for deep-fat frying
  Optional: Thinly sliced green onions and lime wedges

1. Cut wings into 3 sections; discard wing tip sections. In a large saucepan, combine the syrup, chili sauce, lime juice and mustard. Bring to a boil; cook until liquid is reduced to about 1 cup.
2. Meanwhile, in a large shallow dish, combine the flour, salt, paprika and pepper. Add wings a few at a time and toss to coat.
3. In an electric skillet or deep fryer, heat oil to 375°. Fry wings, a few at a time, for 6-8 minutes or until no longer pink, turning once. Drain wings on paper towels. Transfer wings to a large bowl; add the sauce mixture and toss to coat. Serve immediately, with sliced green onions and lime wedges if desired.
Note: Uncooked chicken wing sections (wingettes) may be substituted for whole chicken wings.
1 piece: 142 cal., 8g fat (1g sat. fat), 15mg chol., 198mg sod., 12g carb. (9g sugars, 0 fiber), 5g pro.

PORK & CHIVE
POT STICKERS

**INSPIRED BY
CHICK-FIL-A®, *CHICKEN SALAD*
*COPYCAT CHICKEN SALAD, P. 49***

SPECIALTY SOUPS, SALADS & SANDWICHES

Mix and match these satisfying soups, salads and sandwiches for a well-rounded meal that will have you more excited to eat at home than ever before.

**JALAPENO BURGERS
WITH GORGONZOLA**

DRIVE-THRU CHILI
INSPIRED BY: WENDY'S®, *CLASSIC CHILI*

I don't eat a lot of fast food—but when I do, I try to pick things that are fairly healthy. I found that Wendy's chili is actually one of the healthiest items on its menu. So when I needed to bring chili to a potluck, I tried to re-create Wendy's recipe and got it pretty close.
—Margo Zoerner, Pleasant Prairie, WI

PREP: 20 min. • **COOK:** 1 hour
MAKES: 20 servings (5 qt.)

- 2½ lbs. ground beef
- 2 cups chopped onion
- 1 cup chopped celery
- 3 Tbsp. chili powder
- 1 Tbsp. ground cumin
- 1 tsp. pepper
- 1 can (4 oz.) chopped green chiles
- 1 garlic clove, minced
- 1 can (46 oz.) tomato juice
- 4 cups V8 juice
- 1 can (28 oz.) diced tomatoes, undrained
- 2 cans (16 oz. each) kidney beans, rinsed and drained
- 2 cans (16 oz. each) pink beans or pinto beans, rinsed and drained
  Optional: Sour cream, cubed avocado, shredded cheddar cheese and sliced jalapeno pepper

1. In a large Dutch oven, cook beef over medium heat until no longer pink; drain. Continue to cook until beef is browned, 4-5 minutes longer. Add the onion and celery; cook until tender. Stir in the chili powder, cumin and pepper; cook for 1 minute. Add green chiles and garlic; cook 1 minute longer.
2. Stir in juices and tomatoes. Bring to a boil. Reduce heat; simmer, uncovered, for 20 minutes. Add beans and simmer 20 minutes longer or until thickened to desired consistency. If desired, serve with sour cream, avocado, cheese and jalapeno slices.
Freeze option: Freeze the cooled chili in freezer containers. To use, partially thaw in refrigerator overnight. Heat through in a saucepan, stirring occasionally; add a little water if necessary.
Note: This recipe was tested with Goya Pink Beans (Habichuelas Rosadas). Pinto beans may be substituted if pink beans are difficult to find.
1 cup: 225 cal., 7g fat (3g sat. fat), 35mg chol., 595mg sod., 23g carb. (7g sugars, 6g fiber), 17g pro.

JALAPENO BURGERS WITH GORGONZOLA
INSPIRED BY: RED ROBIN®, *BURNIN' LOVE BURGER*

On a whim, we mixed homemade jalapeno jam into ground beef patties, then topped the burgers with caramelized onions and tangy Gorgonzola cheese. Fabulous!
—Becky Mollenkamp, St. Louis, MO

TAKES: 30 min. • **MAKES:** 4 servings

- 1 Tbsp. canola oil
- 1 tsp. butter
- 1 medium onion, halved and thinly sliced
  Dash salt
  Dash sugar
  BURGERS
- ⅓ cup jalapeno pepper jelly
- ½ tsp. salt
- ¼ tsp. pepper
- 1 lb. ground beef
- 4 hamburger buns, split and toasted
- 2 Tbsp. crumbled Gorgonzola cheese
  Thinly sliced jalapeno pepper, optional

1. In a small skillet, heat oil and butter over medium heat. Add the onion, salt and sugar; cook and stir until the onion is softened, 3-4 minutes. Reduce heat to medium-low; cook for 4-6 minutes or until deep golden brown, stirring onions occasionally.
2. In a large bowl, mix the jelly, salt and pepper. Add beef; mix lightly but thoroughly. Shape mixture into four ½-in.-thick patties.
3. Grill the burgers, covered, over medium heat or broil 4 in. from the heat until a thermometer reads 160°, 4-5 minutes on each side. Serve on buns with caramelized onion, cheese and, if desired, jalapeno slices.
1 burger: 460 cal., 20g fat (7g sat. fat), 76mg chol., 669mg sod., 43g carb. (18g sugars, 2g fiber), 25g pro.

QUESADILLA
BURGER

QUESADILLA BURGER

INSPIRED BY: APPLEBEE'S®,
QUESADILLA BURGER

My niece fell in love with the quesadilla burger from Applebee's and challenged me to make it at home. She says I got pretty darned close to the real thing!
—*James Schend, Pleasant Prairie, WI*

PREP: 15 min. • **COOK:** 20 min.
MAKES: 4 servings

- 1⅓ lbs. ground beef
- ¾ tsp. salt
- ¼ tsp. pepper
- 1 Tbsp. canola oil
- 4 slices pepper jack cheese
- 8 mini flour tortillas
- 2 cups shredded cheddar cheese
- 4 cooked bacon strips, halved
- 4 lettuce leaves
- ½ cup chipotle ranch salad dressing
- ½ cup pico de gallo

1. Shape ground beef into four 5-in.-wide patties. Sprinkle with salt and pepper. In a large skillet, heat oil over medium heat. Add burgers; cook until a thermometer reads 160°, 4-6 minutes on each side. Remove from heat; top with pepper jack cheese. Cover and let stand 5 minutes.
2. Meanwhile, place tortillas on a griddle. Sprinkle ¼ cup cheddar cheese on each tortilla. Cook over low heat until cheese is melted, 1-2 minutes; remove from the heat. Top half the tortillas with burgers, bacon, lettuce, ranch dressing and pico de gallo; top with remaining tortillas, cheese side down.

1 burger: 925 cal., 67g fat (27g sat. fat), 189mg chol., 1640mg sod., 23g carb. (3g sugars, 3g fiber), 53g pro.

HAVE IT YOUR WAY.

For almost all *Taste of Home* recipes using ground beef, we call for an 80/20 blend. This is a good mix of lean meat to fat, so burgers are still juicy. You're free to switch up the kind of beef if you'd like, but know that your burgers may be less juicy and flavorful if you go for a leaner option.

COPYCAT SOUTHWEST CHICKEN SALAD

COPYCAT SOUTHWEST CHICKEN SALAD

INSPIRED BY: APPLEBEE'S®,
SOUTHWESTERN CHICKEN SALAD

My husband and I loved this salad the first time we ate it at Applebee's. After eating it three times, my husband asked for info on the ingredients in the dressing. The waitress told us, so I went home and worked on a version we feel tastes just as delicious.
—*Pamela Shank, Parkersburg, WV*

TAKES: 30 min. • **MAKES:** 2 servings

- ⅓ cup chopped red onion
- ¼ cup pickled jalapeno slices, chopped
- ¼ cup coleslaw salad dressing
- 1 Tbsp. juice from pickled jalapeno slices
- 1 Tbsp. lime juice
- 2 boneless skinless chicken breast halves (6 oz. each)
- ¼ cup frozen corn
- 3 cups chopped romaine
- ¼ cup chopped sweet red pepper
- ¼ cup chopped seeded tomatoes
- ¼ cup canned black beans, rinsed and drained
- ½ cup shredded cheddar cheese
- ½ cup tri-color tortilla strips

1. Place the first 5 ingredients in a jar with a tight-fitting lid; shake contents well. Refrigerate until serving.
2. Place chicken on oiled grill rack. Grill, covered, over medium heat or broil 3 in. from the heat until a thermometer reads 165°, 5-7 minutes on each side. Let stand for 5 minutes before slicing the chicken. Meanwhile, prepare corn according to package directions.
3. Divide the romaine between 2 salad bowls. Arrange chicken over romaine; top with corn, red pepper, tomatoes and beans. Sprinkle with cheese and tortilla strips. Shake the dressing again; drizzle over salads. Serve immediately.

1 salad: 557 cal., 26g fat (8g sat. fat), 132mg chol., 826mg sod., 33g carb. (9g sugars, 4g fiber), 45g pro.

POTATO, SAUSAGE & KALE SOUP

HOW-TO
Soup's On!
1. Fully cook the sausage and onion over medium heat, breaking the meat into crumbles.
2. Add the seasonings, potatoes, kale, milk and cream. Bring to a boil, then simmer until potatoes are tender.
3. Mix cornstarch and water until smooth; stir into soup. Stir constantly until soup returns to a boil; cook and stir until thickened.

POTATO, SAUSAGE & KALE SOUP
INSPIRED BY: OLIVE GARDEN®, ZUPPA TOSCANA

I let my young son pick out seed packets, and he chose kale, which grew like crazy. This hearty soup has helped make good use of it, and it rivals the Olive Garden's Zuppa Toscana.
—*Michelle Babbie, Malone, NY*

TAKES: 30 min. • **MAKES:** 4 servings

- ½ lb. bulk pork sausage
- 1 medium onion, finely chopped
- 2 tsp. chicken bouillon granules
- ½ tsp. garlic powder
- ½ tsp. pepper
- 2 medium red potatoes, cut into ½-in. cubes
- 2 cups sliced fresh kale
- 3 cups 2% milk
- 1 cup heavy whipping cream
- 1 Tbsp. cornstarch
- ¼ cup cold water
  Crumbled cooked bacon, optional

1. In a large saucepan, cook sausage and onion over medium heat 4-6 minutes or until sausage is no longer pink and onion is tender, breaking up the sausage into crumbles; drain.
2. Stir in bouillon and seasonings. Add the potatoes, kale, milk and cream; bring to a boil. Reduce heat; simmer, covered, until potatoes are tender, 10-15 minutes.
3. In a small bowl, mix the cornstarch and water until smooth; stir into soup. Return to a boil, stirring constantly; cook and stir for 1-2 minutes or until thickened. If desired, top with bacon.

1½ cups: 504 cal., 38g fat (20g sat. fat), 128mg chol., 881mg sod., 26g carb. (12g sugars, 2g fiber), 15g pro.

WHY YOU'LL LOVE IT...
"I made this soup exactly as written, and it was amazingly delicious! It may be the best soup I've ever made. It was fast, easy and very tasty!"
—DARLENE2554, TASTEOFHOME.COM

**CINNAMON WHISKEY
BBQ CHICKEN MELT**

STRAWBERRY KALE SALAD
INSPIRED BY: CULVER'S®,
STRAWBERRY FIELDS SALAD

This fresh, zingy salad is super easy and just like the one I get at Culver's! The sliced strawberries and mint give it an extra-summery feel, and bacon and toasted almonds add the perfect amount of crunch.
—*Luanne Asta, Hampton Bays, NY*

TAKES: 25 min. • **MAKES:** 10 servings

- ½ cup olive oil
- ⅓ cup cider vinegar
- 1 tsp. honey
- ¼ tsp. salt
- ⅛ tsp. pepper
- 1 bunch kale (about 12 oz.), trimmed and chopped (about 14 cups)
- 2 cups sliced fresh strawberries
- ¾ lb. bacon strips, cooked and crumbled
- ¼ cup minced fresh mint
- 1 cup crumbled feta cheese
- ¼ cup slivered almonds, toasted

1. For dressing, whisk together the first 5 ingredients.
2. To serve, place kale, strawberries, bacon and mint in a large bowl; toss with dressing. Sprinkle with cheese and almonds.
Note: To toast the nuts, bake in a shallow pan in a 350° oven for 5-10 minutes or cook in a skillet over low heat until lightly browned, stirring occasionally.
1⅓ cups: 231 cal., 19g fat (4g sat. fat), 18mg chol., 399mg sod., 8g carb. (2g sugars, 2g fiber), 8g pro.

CINNAMON WHISKEY
BBQ CHICKEN MELT
INSPIRED BY: UNO PIZZERIA & GRILL®,
WHISKY BBQ CHICKEN SANDWICH

I re-created this sandwich from the Uno Pizzeria & Grill menu. Make the sauce ahead so the sandwiches can come together quickly when the craving hits! I make my sandwiches in a panini press set to medium.
—*Jolene Martinelli, Fremont, NH*

TAKES: 30 min. • **MAKES:** 2 servings

- 4 frozen breaded chicken tenders
- 3 Tbsp. barbecue sauce
- 2 tsp. whiskey
- ¼ tsp. ground cinnamon
- 4 slices sourdough bread
- 4 slices cheddar cheese
- 4 cooked bacon strips
- 2 Tbsp. ranch salad dressing
- 4 tsp. butter, softened

1. Prepare chicken tenders according to package directions. Meanwhile, stir together barbecue sauce, whiskey and cinnamon.
2. Top 2 slices of bread with half the cheddar cheese; add bacon. Place the chicken tenders on top of bacon. Drizzle with barbecue sauce and ranch; top with remaining cheese. Top with remaining bread. Spread outsides of sandwiches with butter.
3. In a skillet over medium heat, toast sandwiches until cheese is melted and outside is golden brown, 2-3 minutes on each side.
1 sandwich: 691 cal., 41g fat (19g sat. fat), 102mg chol., 1626mg sod., 50g carb. (13g sugars, 2g fiber), 29g pro.

COPYCAT COLESLAW

TEQUILA-LIME STEAK SALAD

INSPIRED BY: NUTRIFIT®,
TEQUILA & LIME MARINATED STEAK SALAD
This NutriFit copycat recipe has become one of my family's Fourth of July favorites. The adults can make margaritas from the rest of the tequila!
—Laura Wilhelm, West Hollywood, CA

PREP: 15 min. + marinating
GRILL: 10 min.
MAKES: 6 servings

¾ cup plus 1 Tbsp. lime juice, divided
¾ cup blanco tequila
2 Tbsp. garlic powder
1 Tbsp. ground cumin
1 Tbsp. Montreal steak seasoning
1 Tbsp. dried oregano
½ tsp. pepper
⅛ tsp. crushed red pepper flakes
2 lbs. beef flank steak
1 pkg. (9 to 10 oz.) hearts of romaine salad mix
3 Tbsp. olive oil
1 pint rainbow cherry tomatoes, halved
 Optional: Cotija cheese and lime wedges

1. In a large bowl, whisk together ¾ cup lime juice, tequila, garlic powder, cumin, steak seasoning, oregano, pepper and red pepper flakes. Place the steak in a shallow dish; add tequila mixture and turn to coat. Refrigerate, covered, for 8 hours or overnight, turning once.
2. Drain beef, discarding marinade; pat dry. Grill, covered, over direct medium-high heat, turning once, 10-15 minutes or until the desired degree of doneness (for medium-rare, a thermometer should read 135°; medium, 140°; medium-well, 145°). Place beef on cutting board; cover and let rest 5-10 minutes. Thinly slice steak across the grain.
3. Place salad mix on serving platter; drizzle with the olive oil and remaining 1 Tbsp. lime juice. Place the steak over romaine; top with the tomatoes and, if desired, cotija cheese and lime wedges.
4 oz. cooked steak with 1½ cups salad: 257 cal., 11g fat (5g sat. fat), 72mg chol., 243mg sod., 8g carb. (2g sugars, 2g fiber), 31g pro. **Diabetic exchanges:** 4 lean meat, 1½ fat, 1 vegetable.

COPYCAT COLESLAW

INSPIRED BY: KFC®, *COLESLAW*
We love going to KFC. Although we enjoy the chicken there, we actually go for the coleslaw—and we usually buy several pints at a time. I make several versions of coleslaw, but we sometime just want this. I tried for several years before getting this recipe right. If you are in a hurry, get a bag of preshredded slaw mix. It is not quite as good as grating it yourself, though.
—Donna Gribbins, Shelbyville, KY

PREP: 20 min. + chilling
MAKES: 8 servings

½ cup buttermilk
½ cup mayonnaise
⅓ cup sugar
2 Tbsp. lemon juice
4½ tsp. white vinegar
1 tsp. salt
½ tsp. pepper
1 lb. finely chopped cabbage (about 8 cups)
2 medium carrots, finely chopped (about 2 cups)
3 Tbsp. grated onion

In a large bowl, whisk the first 7 ingredients until combined. Add the remaining ingredients; toss to coat. Refrigerate, covered, at least 2 hours and up to 3 days before serving.
¾ cup: 160 cal., 10g fat (2g sat. fat), 6mg chol., 421mg sod., 16g carb. (13g sugars, 3g fiber), 2g pro.

COPY THAT!

It is completely normal for the cabbage to release water when mixed with the other ingredients in this recipe. This helps contribute to the dressing, and evenly coats the coleslaw. If you don't like so much liquid, you can easily drain it off before serving. Or, better yet, serve this copycat coleslaw with a slotted spoon.

TEQUILA-LIME
STEAK SALAD

CHICKEN PESTO SANDWICHES

CHICKEN PESTO SANDWICHES

INSPIRED BY: PANERA BREAD®, *PESTO CHICKEN SANDWICH*

Years ago I had a pesto chicken sandwich at Panera and fell in love. I haven't seen it on that menu for a long time so I had to create my own version.

—*Colleen Sturma, Milwaukee, WI*

TAKES: 30 min. • **MAKES:** 6 servings

- 6 boneless skinless chicken breast halves (6 oz. each)
- ¾ cup prepared pesto, divided
- ½ tsp. salt
- ¼ tsp. pepper
- 1 jar (12 oz.) roasted sweet red peppers, drained
- 6 Ciabatta buns, split and toasted
- ¼ lb. fresh mozzarella cheese, cut into 6 slices

1. Flatten the chicken to ¼-in. thickness. Spread 1 Tbsp. pesto over each chicken breast; sprinkle with salt and pepper. Grill chicken, covered, over medium heat until no longer pink, 3-5 minutes on each side.

2. Spread 3 Tbsp. pesto over bun bottoms; layer with red peppers, chicken and cheese. Spread remaining pesto over cut side of bun tops; replace tops.

1 sandwich: 498 cal., 22g fat (6g sat. fat), 111mg chol., 1026mg sod., 27g carb. (6g sugars, 1g fiber), 43g pro.

HAVE IT YOUR WAY

If you don't have fresh mozzarella, you can use regular mozzarella or provolone slices. However, we'd recommend going out of your way to pick up some fresh mozzarella, because it makes all the difference!

ARBY'S BEEF & CHEDDAR SLIDERS

ARBY'S BEEF & CHEDDAR SLIDERS

INSPIRED BY: ARBY'S®, *BEEF & CHEDDAR*

These delicious sliders are made from deli roast beef and a copycat Arby's sauce. The recipe is a quick weeknight meal and an amazing replica of the wonderful beef and cheddar sandwich from Arby's. If you like your sandwiches really cheesy, go ahead and add another layer on top of the beef before baking.

—*Claudia Lamascolo, Melbourne, FL*

PREP: 15 min. • **BAKE:** 30 min.
MAKES: 6 servings

- 1 pkg. (12 oz.) Hawaiian sweet rolls
- 14 oz. thinly sliced deli roast beef
- ½ cup barbecue sauce
- 6 slices sharp cheddar cheese
- ¼ cup butter, cubed
- 2 Tbsp. brown sugar
- 2 tsp. Worcestershire sauce
- 2 tsp. prepared mustard
- 1½ tsp. dried minced onion or poppy seeds
- ½ tsp. garlic powder

1. Preheat the oven to 350°. Without separating rolls, cut the package of rolls in half horizontally; arrange the bottom halves in a greased 11x7-in. baking dish. In a bowl, combine roast beef and barbecue sauce. Top with cheese slices. Replace top halves of rolls.

2. In a small skillet, melt butter over medium heat. Whisk in brown sugar, Worcestershire sauce, mustard, dried minced onion and garlic powder. Cook and stir until sugar is dissolved; drizzle over sandwiches.

3. Cover; bake 25 minutes. Uncover; bake until golden brown, 5-10 minutes longer.

2 sliders: 335 cal., 20g fat (13g sat. fat), 78mg chol., 587mg sod., 25g carb. (12g sugars, 1g fiber), 16g pro.

SUMMER STRAWBERRY SALAD
INSPIRED BY: PANERA BREAD®, *STRAWBERRY POPPYSEED SALAD*

I love the Strawberry Poppyseed Salad at Panera but can't always make it to the restaurant, so I created my own version. It's quick, delicious and ready whenever I want it.
—*Diane Marie Sahley, Lakewood, OH*

TAKES: 15 min. • **MAKES:** 4 servings

1 pkg. (10 oz.) romaine salad mix (about 8 cups)
1 lb. sliced cooked chicken
1½ cups sliced fresh strawberries
1 cup pineapple tidbits, drained
½ cup mandarin oranges, drained
½ cup fresh blueberries
½ cup chopped pecans
½ cup poppy seed salad dressing

Arrange romaine on 4 serving plates. Top with the chicken, strawberries, pineapple, mandarin oranges and blueberries. Sprinkle with chopped pecans. Drizzle with dressing.
2 cups: 557 cal., 31g fat (5g sat. fat), 111mg chol., 329mg sod., 34g carb. (25g sugars, 5g fiber), 37g pro.

HONEY CHIPOTLE VINAIGRETTE
INSPIRED BY: CHIPOTLE MEXICAN GRILL®, *CHIPOTLE-HONEY VINAIGRETTE*

We've all been there. It's 7 p.m. and you're at home with a sudden craving for Chipotle. You don't feel like going all the way to Chipotle—they don't have a drive-thru anyway—and delivery is kind of slow. What's a hungry person to do? You make an at-home Chipotle salad complete with a copycat version of its Honey Chipotle Vinaigrette! It's one of our favorite homemade salad dressings.
—*Lauren Habermehl, Pewaukee, WI*

TAKES: 15 min. • **MAKES:** 1 cup

⅓ cup red wine vinegar
3 Tbsp. honey
1 chipotle pepper in adobo sauce
1½ tsp. adobo sauce
1 tsp. garlic powder
1 tsp. ground cumin
¾ tsp. salt
½ tsp. dried oregano
¼ tsp. pepper
½ cup extra virgin olive oil

In a blender or food processor, combine first 9 ingredients; puree until smooth. With the motor running, slowly drizzle in olive oil.
2 Tbsp.: 152 cal., 14g fat (2g sat. fat), 0 chol., 253mg sod., 8g carb. (7g sugars, 0 fiber), 0 pro.

LETTUCE WRAPS
INSPIRED BY: P.F. CHANG'S®, *LETTUCE WRAPS*

Enjoy these light but filling restaurant faves from the comfort of your own home.
—*Kendra Doss, Colorado Springs, CO*

TAKES: 25 min. • **MAKES:** 6 servings

1 Tbsp. plus 1½ tsp. peanut oil, divided
1½ lbs. boneless skinless chicken breasts, cubed
¾ cup chopped fresh mushrooms
1 can (8 oz.) water chestnuts, drained and diced
1 Tbsp. minced fresh gingerroot
2 Tbsp. rice vinegar
2 Tbsp. reduced-sodium teriyaki sauce
1 Tbsp. reduced-sodium soy sauce
½ tsp. garlic powder
¼ tsp. crushed red pepper flakes
½ cup julienned green onions
12 Bibb or Boston lettuce leaves

1. In a large nonstick skillet, heat 1 Tbsp. oil over medium-high heat. Add chicken. Cook and stir for 3 minutes; drain. Add mushrooms, water chestnuts and ginger; cook until the chicken is no longer pink, 4-6 minutes longer. Drain and set aside.
2. In a small bowl, whisk vinegar, teriyaki sauce, soy sauce, garlic powder, red pepper flakes and remaining 1½ tsp. oil. Stir in onions and the chicken mixture.
3. Spoon onto lettuce leaves. If desired, fold sides of lettuce over the filling and roll up.
2 wraps: 232 cal., 13g fat (3g sat. fat), 75mg chol., 641mg sod., 11g carb. (5g sugars, 2g fiber), 20g pro.

COPYCAT FRIED CHICKEN SANDWICH

COPYCAT FRIED CHICKEN SANDWICH
INSPIRED BY: POPEYES®,
CLASSIC CHICKEN SANDWICH

After trying all the major fast food chain's chicken sandwiches, I decided to come up with my own version. I know everyone says theirs is better than the original, but mine really is.
—*Ralph Jones, San Diego, CA*

PREP: 15 min. + marinating
COOK: 20 min./batch • **MAKES:** 6 servings

- 3   boneless skinless chicken breast halves (6 oz. each)
- ¾   cup buttermilk
- 2   tsp. hot pepper sauce
- 2   large eggs, beaten
- 2   cups all-purpose flour
- 1   Tbsp. plus 1 tsp. garlic powder
- 1   Tbsp. each onion powder and paprika
- 2   tsp. pepper
- 1   tsp. salt
- ⅓   cup canola oil
- 6   brioche hamburger buns, split
      Optional: Shredded lettuce, sliced tomatoes, pickle slices, onion slices, mayonnaise

1. Cut each chicken breast horizontally in half; place in a large bowl. Add buttermilk and hot sauce; toss to coat. Refrigerate, covered, 8 hours or overnight.

2. Preheat air fryer to 400°. Stir eggs into the chicken mixture. In a shallow dish, whisk the flour, garlic powder, onion powder, paprika, pepper and salt. Remove chicken from buttermilk mixture. Dredge the chicken in flour mixture, firmly patting to help coating adhere. Repeat, dipping the chicken again in buttermilk mixture and then dredging in flour mixture.

3. Place chicken on a wire rack over a baking sheet. Refrigerate, uncovered, for 30 minutes. Using a pastry brush, lightly dab both sides of chicken with oil until no dry breading remains.

4. In batches, arrange chicken in a single layer on greased tray in air-fryer basket. Cook until a thermometer reads 165° and coating is golden brown and crispy, 7-8 minutes on each side. Remove the chicken; keep warm. Toast buns in air fryer until golden brown, 2-3 minutes. Top bun bottoms with chicken. If desired, serve with optional toppings. Replace bun tops.

Note: In our testing, we find cook times vary dramatically among brands of air fryers. As a result, we give wider than normal ranges on suggested cook times. Begin checking at the first time listed and adjust as needed.

1 sandwich: 384 cal., 17g fat (3g sat. fat), 136mg chol., 777mg sod., 31g carb. (8g sugars, 3g fiber), 26g pro.

COPYCAT CHICKEN SALAD
INSPIRED BY: CHICK-FIL-A®, *CHICKEN SALAD*

Inspired by Chick-fil-A chicken salad, this recipe is incredibly easy to make, and your family will love it. The sweet pickle relish gives it that signature taste. I like to use a thick crusty oat bread.
—*Julie Peterson, Crofton, MD*

TAKES: 20 min. • **MAKES:** 2 servings

- ½   cup reduced-fat mayonnaise
- ⅓   cup sweet pickle relish
- ⅓   cup finely chopped celery
- ½   tsp. sugar
- ¼   tsp. salt
- ¼   tsp. pepper
- 1   hard-boiled large egg, cooled and minced
- 2   cups chopped cooked chicken breast
- 4   slices whole wheat bread, toasted
- 2   romaine leaves

Mix the first 7 ingredients; stir in chicken. Line 2 slices of toast with the lettuce. Top with chicken salad and remaining toast.

1 sandwich: 651 cal., 29g fat (5g sat. fat), 222mg chol., 1386mg sod., 45g carb. (18g sugars, 4g fiber), 51g pro.

HAVE IT YOUR WAY.

If you're cooking your own chicken for this recipe, you'll need roughly a pound of raw chicken breasts to get 2 cups of chopped cooked breast meat.

INSPIRED BY
CAFE RIO'S®,
SWEET PORK

*CAFE RIO COPYCAT
PORK BOWLS, P. 60*

COPYCAT ENTREES

Serve up signature dishes from your favorite eateries with these easy-to-assemble recipes that bring tasty takeout to the dining room table.

SKILLET-GRILLED CATFISH
INSPIRED BY: CRACKER BARREL®,
U.S. FARM-RAISED CATFISH

You can use this recipe with any thick fish fillet, but I suggest using catfish or haddock. The Cajun flavor is great.
—*Traci Wynne, Denver, PA*

TAKES: 25 min. • **MAKES:** 4 servings

- ¼ cup all-purpose flour
- ¼ cup cornmeal
- 1 tsp. onion powder
- 1 tsp. dried basil
- ½ tsp. garlic salt
- ½ tsp. dried thyme
- ¼ to ½ tsp. white pepper
- ¼ to ½ tsp. cayenne pepper
- ¼ to ½ tsp. pepper
- 4 catfish fillets (6 to 8 oz. each)
- ¼ cup butter
  Optional: Lemon wedges and minced fresh parsley

1. In a large shallow dish, combine the first 9 ingredients. Add catfish, 1 fillet at a time, and turn to coat.
2. Place a large cast-iron skillet on a grill rack over medium-high heat. Melt butter in the skillet; add catfish in batches, if necessary. Grill, covered, 5-10 minutes on each side or until fish just begins to flake easily with a fork. If desired, serve with lemon wedges and fresh parsley.
1 fillet: 222 cal., 15g fat (8g sat. fat), 51mg chol., 366mg sod., 14g carb. (0 sugars, 1g fiber), 8g pro.

COPYCAT HONEY BAKED HAM

COPYCAT HONEY BAKED HAM
INSPIRED BY: THE HONEY BAKED HAM COMPANY®, *HONEY BAKED HAM*

For holidays and special occasions my family loves a good old-fashioned baked ham. One year I decided to see if I could duplicate the crunchy glaze on a Honey Baked Ham. After tweaking the recipe a couple of times I developed a pretty good imitation. If you have a kitchen torch, you can torch the sugar instead of broiling it. That method is just as easy.
—*Donna Gribbins, Shelbyville, KY*

PREP: 10 min.
COOK: 4 hours 5 min. + standing
MAKES: 16 servings

- 1 spiral-sliced fully cooked bone-in ham (8 to 10 lbs.)
- 1 cup water
- ¾ cup honey, divided

GLAZE
- 1 cup sugar
- ½ tsp. ground cinnamon
- ½ tsp. ground allspice
- ½ tsp. pepper
- ½ tsp. paprika
- ¼ tsp. ground ginger
- ¼ tsp. ground nutmeg
- ¼ tsp. ground mustard
- ¼ tsp. Chinese five-spice powder
- ⅛ tsp. ground cloves

1. Place the ham and water in a 7-qt. slow cooker. Brush ham with ½ cup honey. Cook, covered, on low until a thermometer reads 140°, 4 to 5 hours.
2. Preheat broiler. Combine the glaze ingredients. Transfer ham to a rack in a shallow roasting pan, cut side down. Brush with the remaining ¼ cup honey; sprinkle with glaze mixture, pressing to adhere. Broil 6-8 in. from heat until lightly browned and the sugar is melted, 3-5 minutes, rotating as needed. Cover with foil; let stand until glaze hardens, about 30 minutes.
5 oz. cooked ham: 288 cal., 6g fat (2g sat. fat), 100mg chol., 1192mg sod., 26g carb. (26g sugars, 0 fiber), 33g pro.

EASY HONEY MUSTARD CHICKEN

COPYCAT CHEESY GORDITA CRUNCH

INSPIRED BY: TACO BELL®, *GORDITA CRUNCH*
Skip the drive-thru line and enjoy these fast-food favorites any time!
—Taste of Home *Test Kitchen*

TAKES: 25 min. • **MAKES:** 8 servings

- 1 lb. ground beef
- 1 envelope taco seasoning
- ⅔ cup water
- 2 cups shredded cheddar cheese
- 8 flour tortillas (6 in.)
- 8 taco shells, warmed
- 8 Tbsp. spicy ranch salad dressing
  Optional toppings: Shredded cheddar cheese, sour cream, shredded lettuce, diced tomatoes, chopped red onion and lime wedges

1. In a large skillet skillet, cook the beef over medium heat until no longer pink, 5-7 minutes, breaking beef into crumbles; drain. Stir in taco seasoning and water. Bring to a boil. Reduce heat; simmer, uncovered, for 2-3 minutes or until thickened.
2. Meanwhile, sprinkle ¼ cup cheese over 1 side of each tortilla. Place on a microwave-safe plate; heat, uncovered, on high 15-20 seconds or until cheese is melted. Immediately wrap each tortilla around a taco shell. Fill with the beef mixture. Drizzle with the spicy ranch dressing. Serve with the toppings of your choice.
1 taco: 357 cal., 22g fat (9g sat. fat), 60mg chol., 929mg sod., 22g carb. (2g sugars, 1g fiber), 18g pro.

EASY HONEY MUSTARD CHICKEN

INSPIRED BY: BAKERS SQUARE®,
HONEY MUSTARD CHICKEN
My absolute favorite dish at Bakers Square is the Honey Mustard Chicken. Unfortunately, the Bakers Square near me relocated. So, I devised this version, which is quick and easy.
—*Arlene Erlbach, Morton Grove, IL*

PREP: 15 min. • **COOK:** 25 min.
MAKES: 4 servings

- ¾ cup Dijon honey mustard salad dressing
- ⅓ cup chicken broth
- ⅓ cup half-and-half cream
- ¼ tsp. salt
- ¼ tsp. pepper
- ¼ cup all-purpose flour
- 4 boneless skinless chicken breast halves (6 oz. each)
- 3 Tbsp. olive oil, divided
- ½ lb. medium fresh mushrooms, thinly sliced
- 1 large sweet onion, halved and thinly sliced

1. In a small bowl, combine the first 5 ingredients. Place flour in a shallow bowl. Add chicken, a few pieces at a time, and toss to coat; shake off excess. In a large skillet, heat 2 Tbsp. oil over medium-high heat. Brown chicken on both sides. Remove. In same pan, cook mushrooms and onion in remaining 1 Tbsp. oil until tender, 6-8 minutes.
2. Add the dressing mixture, stirring to loosen browned bits from pan. Return chicken to pan; bring to a boil. Reduce the heat; simmer, uncovered, until a thermometer inserted in the chicken reads 165°, 12-15 minutes longer.
1 serving: 563 cal., 35g fat (6g sat. fat), 117mg chol., 548mg sod., 23g carb. (12g sugars, 1g fiber), 38g pro.

WHY YOU'LL LOVE IT ...

"Everyone loved this dish. I made no changes, and it doesn't need any!"
—DEBBRA932, TASTEOFHOME.COM

CRISPY FRIED CHICKEN

KUNG PAO CHICKEN

INSPIRED BY: PANDA EXPRESS®,
KUNG PAO CHICKEN

My family loves the kung pao chicken from our favorite Chinese restaurant. But in less time than it takes for the delivery to arrive, we can be digging into a platter of this copycat recipe!
—*Jennifer Beckman, Falls Church, VA*

PREP: 25 min. • **COOK:** 15 min.
MAKES: 4 servings

- 1 lb. boneless skinless chicken breasts, cut into ¾-in. cubes
- 3 tsp. cornstarch, divided
- ½ tsp. salt
- ½ tsp. pepper
- 2 Tbsp. chicken stock
- 2 Tbsp. hoisin sauce
- 1 Tbsp. reduced-sodium soy sauce
- 1 Tbsp. oyster sauce
- ½ tsp. Sriracha chili sauce or ¼ tsp. hot pepper sauce
- 2 Tbsp. peanut oil, divided
- 1 small red onion, chopped
- 1 medium sweet red pepper, chopped
- 2 garlic cloves, minced
- 1 tsp. minced fresh gingerroot
- ¼ cup minced fresh cilantro
- ¼ cup dry roasted peanuts

1. In a large bowl, combine chicken, 1 tsp. cornstarch, salt and pepper.
2. Place remaining 2 tsp. cornstarch in a small bowl. Stir in the stock, hoisin sauce, soy sauce, oyster sauce and chili sauce until smooth.
3. In a large skillet or wok, stir-fry the chicken in batches in 1 Tbsp. oil until no longer pink. Remove and keep warm.
4. Stir-fry the onion and red pepper in remaining 1 Tbsp. oil for 2-5 minutes or until vegetables are crisp-tender. Add garlic and ginger; cook 1 minute longer.
5. Stir cornstarch mixture and add to the pan. Bring to a boil; cook and stir for 2 minutes or until thickened. Add chicken; heat through. Stir in cilantro and peanuts.
¾ cup: 285 cal., 14g fat (3g sat. fat), 63mg chol., 857mg sod., 13g carb. (5g sugars, 2g fiber), 26g pro.

CRISPY FRIED CHICKEN

INSPIRED BY: KFC®,
ORIGINAL RECIPE CHICKEN

This fried chicken can be served hot or pulled out of the fridge the next day as leftovers. Either way, folks love it.
—*Jeanne Schnitzler, Lima, MT*

PREP: 15 min. • **COOK:** 15 min./batch
MAKES: 12 servings

- 4 cups all-purpose flour, divided
- 2 Tbsp. garlic salt
- 1 Tbsp. paprika
- 3 tsp. pepper, divided
- 2½ tsp. poultry seasoning
- 2 large eggs
- 1½ cups water
- 1 tsp. salt
- 2 broiler/fryer chickens (3½ to 4 lbs. each), cut up
  Oil for deep-fat frying

1. In a large shallow dish, combine 2⅔ cups flour, garlic salt, paprika, 2½ tsp. pepper and poultry seasoning. In another shallow dish, beat eggs and 1½ cups water, then add salt and the remaining 1⅓ cups flour and ½ tsp. pepper. Dip chicken in egg mixture, then place in flour mixture, a few pieces at a time. Turn to coat.
2. In a deep-fat fryer, heat oil to 375°. Fry chicken, several pieces at a time, until the chicken is golden brown and juices run clear, 7-8 minutes on each side. Drain on paper towels.
5 oz. cooked chicken: 543 cal., 33g fat (7g sat. fat), 137mg chol., 798mg sod., 17g carb. (0 sugars, 1g fiber), 41g pro.

COPY THAT!

A thrifty alternative to purchased garlic salt is to mix up your own. Just combine 1 tsp. garlic powder with 3 tsp. table salt or other fine-grained salt. The ratio works the same for onion salt too.

KUNG PAO
CHICKEN

SEASONED CHICKEN STRIPS

INSPIRED BY: WENDY'S®, *CHICKEN TENDERS*

I made these crisp chicken strips for my kids, but they're tasty for company, too.
—*Becky Oliver, Fairplay, CO*

TAKES: 25 min. • **MAKES:** 4 servings

- ⅓ cup egg substitute or 1 large egg
- 1 Tbsp. prepared mustard
- 1 garlic clove, minced
- ¾ cup dry bread crumbs
- 2 tsp. dried basil
- 1 tsp. paprika
- ½ tsp. salt
- ¼ tsp. pepper
- 1 lb. chicken tenderloins

1. Preheat oven to 400°. In a shallow bowl, whisk together egg substitute, mustard and garlic. In another shallow bowl, toss the bread crumbs with the seasonings. Dip chicken in egg mixture, then coat with crumb mixture.
2. Place on a baking sheet coated with cooking spray. Bake for 10-15 minutes or until golden brown and chicken is no longer pink.

3 oz. cooked chicken: 194 cal., 2g fat (0 sat. fat), 56mg chol., 518mg sod., 14g carb. (1g sugars, 1g fiber), 31g pro. **Diabetic exchanges:** 3 lean meat, 1 starch.

KING BURGERS

KING BURGERS

INSPIRED BY: BURGER KING®, *STUFFED STEAKHOUSE BURGER*

My husband is a grill master, and we make up recipes together. The sauce for this juicy burger tastes even better when it's been refrigerated overnight.
—*Mary Potter, Sterling Heights, MI*

TAKES: 30 min. • **MAKES:** 6 servings

- 2 Tbsp. butter
- ¼ cup mayonnaise
- 2 Tbsp. prepared horseradish
- 2 Tbsp. Dijon mustard
- ⅛ tsp. salt
- ⅛ tsp. pepper

BURGERS
- 1½ lbs. ground beef
- ⅓ cup beef broth
- 2½ tsp. hamburger seasoning, divided
- 6 hamburger buns, split
- 3 Tbsp. butter, softened
  Optional: Shredded lettuce, sliced tomato and red onion

1. Cut 2 Tbsp. butter into 6 slices; let remaining butter soften. Place slices in a single layer on a small plate; freeze until firm. For sauce, in a small bowl, mix mayonnaise, horseradish, mustard, salt and pepper until blended.
2. In a large bowl, combine beef, broth and 1½ tsp. hamburger seasoning; mix lightly but thoroughly. Shape beef into 6 patties. Place a butter slice in the center of each; shape the beef around the butter, forming ¾-in.-thick patties. Sprinkle patties with remaining 1 tsp. hamburger seasoning.
3. Grill burgers, covered, over medium heat 5-7 minutes on each side or until a thermometer reads 160°. Spread buns with softened butter. Grill the buns over medium heat for 30-60 seconds, cut side down, until toasted. Serve burgers on buns with sauce and toppings.

Freeze option: Place the patties on a foil-lined baking sheet; wrap and freeze until firm. Remove from pan and transfer to a freezer container; return to freezer. To use, cook frozen patties as directed, increasing the time as necessary for a thermometer to read 160°.

1 burger: 482 cal., 32g fat (12g sat. fat), 99mg chol., 822mg sod., 23g carb. (3g sugars, 1g fiber), 25g pro.

COPYCAT
CHEESECAKE
FACTORY
CHICKEN
PICCATA

COPYCAT CHEESECAKE FACTORY CHICKEN PICCATA

INSPIRED BY: CHEESECAKE FACTORY®, *CHICKEN PICCATA*

In a quest to encourage my six children to eat healthfully, I'm always on the prowl for ways to transform items that usually are received with turned-up, wrinkled noses, into ones that even the pickiest of eaters won't complain about. A smile of satisfaction from my table of hungry eaters is the best payback I can receive. It lets me hang my mama-super-hero-cape up once again at the end of the night!
—*Michelle Stillman, Lancaster, PA*

PREP: 20 min. • **COOK:** 30 min.
MAKES: 4 servings

- 12 oz. uncooked angel hair pasta
- 4 boneless skinless chicken breast halves (6 oz. each)
- ½ cup all-purpose flour
- 1¼ tsp. salt, divided
- ¾ tsp. pepper, divided
- 2 Tbsp. olive oil, divided
- 4 Tbsp. butter, divided
- ¾ lb. sliced fresh mushrooms
- 1 cup dry white wine or chicken broth
- 2 Tbsp. lemon juice
- ½ cup heavy whipping cream
- 4 tsp. capers, drained
- 1 Tbsp. minced fresh parsley
  Optional: Lemon slices and Parmesan cheese

1. Cook the angel hair pasta according to package directions.
2. Flatten chicken to ¼-in. thickness. In a shallow bowl, mix flour, ¾ tsp. salt and ½ tsp. pepper. Dip chicken in flour mixture to coat both sides; shake off the excess.
3. In a large skillet, heat 1 Tbsp. oil and 2 Tbsp. butter over medium heat; add chicken. Cook until chicken juices run clear, 3-5 minutes on each side. Remove and keep warm.
4. In same pan, heat remaining 2 Tbsp. butter and 1 Tbsp. oil over medium heat; add the mushrooms. Cook and stir until tender, 5-7 minutes. Add wine and lemon juice, stirring to loosen the browned bits from pan. Bring to a boil; cook until liquid is reduced by about half, 5-7 minutes. Reduce the heat to low. Stir in cream, capers and remaining ½ tsp. salt and ¼ tsp. pepper; heat through.
5. Drain pasta. Serve chicken with the pasta and sauce. Sprinkle with parsley and, if desired, serve with lemon and Parmesan cheese.

1 chicken breast with ½ cup sauce and 1½ cups pasta: 865 cal., 35g fat (17g sat. fat), 158mg chol., 998mg sod., 81g carb. (5g sugars, 4g fiber), 51g pro.

HOW-TO

Piccata-Making Pointers

- Cover the chicken breasts with plastic wrap before flattening for easy cleanup.
- Set floured chicken on a nearby sheet pan.
- Move the chicken only to flip it in the pan. This creates a golden crust on the outside of the chicken.

CHIPOTLE
CHICKEN

CHIPOTLE CHICKEN

INSPIRED BY: CHIPOTLE MEXICAN GRILL®,
MARINATED CHICKEN

No need to make a trip to the famous chain Chipotle for their marinated chicken! Make this easy, flavor-packed grilled chicken at home and prepare for compliments! The smoky, savory marinade with a spicy kick and slightly sweet finish is addictive and tastes just like the restaurant's version! Kids and adults alike love this chicken in bowls, tacos and burritos.

—*Kim Tower, Danville, CA*

PREP: 20 min. + marinating
GRILL: 15 min. + standing
MAKES: 8 servings

- ¼ cup water
- 3 Tbsp. brown sugar
- 3 Tbsp. white vinegar
- 3 Tbsp. canola oil
- 1 Tbsp. chopped chipotle pepper in adobo sauce
- 5 garlic cloves, halved
- 1 Tbsp. ground chipotle pepper or ground ancho chile pepper
- 2½ tsp. ground cumin
- 2½ tsp. dried oregano
- 1½ tsp. kosher salt
- 1 tsp. smoked paprika
- ½ tsp. pepper
- 3 lbs. boneless skinless chicken thighs

1. Place first 12 ingredients in a blender; cover and process until pureed. Transfer the marinade to a large bowl or shallow dish. Add chicken to marinade; turn to coat. Refrigerate 8 hours or overnight.
2. Drain chicken, discarding marinade. Grill the chicken, covered, over medium-high heat or broil 4 in. from heat until a thermometer reads 170°, 6-8 minutes on each side. Let rest for 10 minutes before slicing.
Freeze option: Place cooled chicken in freezer containers. To use, partially thaw in refrigerator overnight. Microwave, covered, on high in a microwave-safe dish until heated through, stirring gently.
4 oz. cooked chicken: 284 cal., 15g fat (4g sat. fat), 113mg chol., 297mg sod., 4g carb. (3g sugars, 0 fiber), 32g pro.
Diabetic exchanges: 4 lean meat, 2 fat.

GARLIC-LEMON
SHRIMP LINGUINE

GARLIC-LEMON SHRIMP LINGUINE

INSPIRED BY: CHEESECAKE FACTORY®,
LEMON SHRIMP LINGUINE

The Cheesecake Factory has an extensive menu, but I always seem to order their delicious, fresh and citrusy Lemon Shrimp Linguine. I'd enjoyed it enough times that I was confident I could reproduce it to share with friends and family. I think I hit it spot on! When I have fresh basil from the garden, I use that instead of parsley.

—*Trisha Kruse, Eagle, ID*

TAKES: 30 min. • **MAKES:** 4 servings

- 8 oz. uncooked linguine
- 2 Tbsp. olive oil
- 1 Tbsp. butter
- 1 lb. uncooked shrimp (26-30 per lb.), peeled and deveined
- 3 garlic cloves, minced
- 1 Tbsp. grated lemon zest
- 1 Tbsp. lemon juice
- 1 tsp. lemon-pepper seasoning
- 2 Tbsp. minced fresh parsley

1. Cook linguine according to package directions for al dente. Meanwhile, in a large skillet, heat oil and butter over medium-high heat. Add shrimp; cook and stir 3 minutes. Add the lemon zest, juice, garlic and lemon pepper; cook and stir for 2-3 minutes longer or until shrimp turn pink. Stir in parsley.
2. Drain linguine, reserving ⅓ cup pasta water. Add enough reserved pasta water to the shrimp mixture to achieve desired consistency. Serve with linguine.
1 serving: 387 cal., 12g fat (3g sat. fat), 146mg chol., 239mg sod., 43g carb. (2g sugars, 2g fiber), 26g pro.

WHY YOU'LL LOVE IT ...

"This is so easy to make! The lemon garlic sauce is fresh and bright, which is a nice change from heavy pasta sauces. This is a new favorite for my weeknight dinner rotation."
—SUSAN8352, TASTEOFHOME.COM

CHICKEN-FRIED STEAK & GRAVY

CAFE RIO COPYCAT PORK BOWLS
INSPIRED BY: CAFE RIO'S®, *SWEET PORK*

My friends are very big fans of Cafe Rio's sweet pork tacos, so I came up with this fake-out to eat in the comfort of our own homes. Serve the pork in flour tortillas or taco shells, or enjoy it on its own.
—*Donna Gribbins, Shelbyville, KY*

PREP: 20 min. + marinating
COOK: 10 hours • **MAKES:** 8 servings

- 2 cans (12 oz. each) cola, divided
- 1 cup packed brown sugar, divided
- 1 bone-in pork shoulder roast (5 to 7 lbs.)
- 1 Tbsp. kosher salt
- 1 Tbsp. garlic powder
- 1 Tbsp. onion powder
- 1 tsp. pepper
- 1½ cups enchilada sauce
- 1 can (7 oz.) chopped green chiles
  Hot cooked rice, optional
  Optional toppings: Black beans, chopped red onion, crumbled Cotija cheese and salsa

1. In a large bowl or shallow dish, combine 1 can cola and ½ cup brown sugar. Add pork; turn to coat. Cover and refrigerate 8 hours or overnight.
2. Drain the pork, discarding marinade. Place pork in a 5- or 6-qt. slow cooker. Add salt, garlic powder, onion powder, pepper and remaining can of cola. Cook, covered, on low until the meat is tender, 8-10 hours.
3. Set meat aside until cool enough to handle. Remove the meat from bones; discard bones. Shred meat with 2 forks. Discard cooking juices and return meat to slow cooker. Stir in enchilada sauce, green chiles and remaining ½ cup brown sugar. Cook, covered, on low until heated through, about 2 hours.
4. Serve pork in bowls over rice with toppings as desired.
Freeze option: Freeze cooled meat mixture in freezer containers. To use, partially thaw in refrigerator overnight. Heat through in a saucepan, stirring mixture occasionally.
1 cup cooked pork: 419 cal., 22g fat (8g sat. fat), 125mg chol., 560mg sod., 18g carb. (15g sugars, 0 fiber), 37g pro.

CHICKEN-FRIED STEAK & GRAVY
INSPIRED BY: CRACKER BARREL®, *COUNTRY FRIED STEAK*

I learned from my grandmother how to make these chicken-fried steaks. I taught my daughters, and when my granddaughters are older, I'll show them, too.
—*Donna Cater, Fort Ann, NY*

TAKES: 30 min. • **MAKES:** 4 servings

- 1¼ cups all-purpose flour, divided
- 2 large eggs
- 1½ cups 2% milk, divided
- 4 beef cubed steaks (6 oz. each)
- 1¼ tsp. salt, divided
- 1 tsp. pepper, divided
  Oil for frying
- 1 cup water

1. Place 1 cup flour in a shallow bowl. In a separate shallow bowl, whisk eggs and ½ cup milk until blended. Sprinkle steaks with ¾ tsp. each salt and pepper. Dip in flour to coat both sides; shake off the excess. Dip in the egg mixture, then again in flour.
2. In a large cast-iron or other heavy skillet, heat ¼ in. oil over medium heat. Add steaks; cook until golden brown and a thermometer reads 160°, 4-6 minutes on each side. Remove from pan; drain on paper towels. Keep warm.
3. Remove all but 2 Tbsp. oil from pan. Stir in the remaining ¼ cup flour, ½ tsp. salt and ¼ tsp. pepper until smooth; cook and stir over medium heat until golden brown, 3-4 minutes. Gradually whisk in the water and remaining 1 cup milk. Bring to a boil, stirring constantly; cook and stir until thickened, 1-2 minutes. Serve with the steaks.
1 steak with ⅓ cup gravy: 563 cal., 28g fat (5g sat. fat), 148mg chol., 839mg sod., 29g carb. (4g sugars, 1g fiber), 46g pro.

DID YOU KNOW?

It's safe for chicken-fried steak to be a little pink. The thinner your steak, the faster it will cook, though. So by the time you get a nice golden brown exterior, your steak might already be cooked through.

CAFE RIO COPYCAT
PORK BOWLS

SMOTHERED CHICKEN
INSPIRED BY: OUTBACK STEAKHOUSE®,
ALICE SPRINGS CHICKEN

I top tender chicken breasts with mushrooms, bacon, green onions and cheese for a comforting meal that's become a family favorite.
—*Penny Walton, Westerville, OH*

TAKES: 20 min. • **MAKES:** 4 servings

- 4 boneless skinless chicken breast halves (5 oz. each)
- ¼ tsp. seasoned salt
- ¼ tsp. garlic powder
- 3 tsp. canola oil, divided
- 1 cup sliced fresh mushrooms
- 1 cup shredded Mexican cheese blend
- 4 green onions, chopped
- 6 bacon strips, cooked and chopped

1. Pound the chicken breasts to ¼-in. thickness. Sprinkle with seasonings.
2. In a large nonstick skillet, heat 1 tsp. oil over medium-high heat; saute mushrooms until tender, 2-3 minutes. Remove from pan.
3. In same pan, cook chicken in remaining 2 tsp. oil until bottoms are browned, about 4 minutes. Turn chicken; top with mushrooms and the remaining ingredients. Cook, covered, until chicken is no longer pink, 4-5 minutes.
1 chicken breast half: 363 cal., 21g fat (7g sat. fat), 116mg chol., 555mg sod., 3g carb. (1g sugars, 1g fiber), 40g pro.

GRILLED LAMB WITH MINT-PEPPER JELLY

GRILLED LAMB WITH MINT-PEPPER JELLY
INSPIRED BY: FOGO DE CHÃO®,
LAMB CHOP RACK WITH MINT JELLY

It's not on the menu, but if you go to Fogo de Chão, make sure you ask for the mint jelly they serve with their rack of lamb. It's divine! This is my version using zippy jalapeno pepper jelly, and it paid off big time. This is a great way to get people who aren't fans of lamb to enjoy it.
—*Lori Stefanishion, Drumheller, AB*

PREP: 15 min. + marinating
GRILL: 30 min. + standing
MAKES: 4 servings

- 2 racks of lamb (1½ lbs. each), trimmed
- 3 Tbsp. Greek seasoning
- ¼ cup balsamic vinegar
- ¼ cup olive oil
- 2 Tbsp. lemon juice
- 2 Tbsp. soy sauce
- 3 garlic cloves, minced
- ½ cup fresh mint leaves, minced
- ½ cup mild jalapeno pepper jelly
- 1 Tbsp. hot water
  Chopped fresh oregano

1. Rub the lamb with Greek seasoning. Refrigerate, covered, for 2 hours. In a shallow bowl, whisk the vinegar, oil, lemon juice, soy sauce and garlic until combined. Add lamb and turn to coat. Refrigerate, covered, for 4-6 hours or overnight, turning once or twice.
2. In a small bowl, mix mint, jelly and hot water until combined. Refrigerate, covered, until serving.
3. Drain lamb, discarding marinade in dish. Cover rib ends of lamb with foil. Grill, covered, on an oiled rack, over direct medium-high heat 2 minutes on each side. Turn; move to indirect heat. Cook, covered, until the meat reaches desired doneness (for medium-rare, a thermometer should read 135°; medium, 140°; medium-well, 145°), 25-30 minutes longer. Let stand for 10 minutes before serving with sauce; sprinkle with fresh oregano and additional fresh mint.
½ rack with 4 Tbsp. sauce: 471 cal., 24g fat (7g sat. fat), 99mg chol., 1841mg sod., 33g carb. (24g sugars, 1g fiber), 31g pro.

FISH & FRIES

SHRIMP TEMPURA
INSPIRED BY: PANDA EXPRESS®,
FRESH TEMPURA SHRIMP

One of my go-to dishes at a local
Chinese restaurant is their shrimp
tempura. It's crispy, delicate and
oh-so delicious.
—*Sarah Tramonte, Milwaukee, WI*

PREP: 15 min. • **COOK:** 20 min.
MAKES: 26 servings

- ¾ cup all-purpose flour
- 6 Tbsp. cornstarch
- 2¼ Tbsp. baking soda
- ½ tsp. salt
- ¾ cold cup club soda
- 1 lb. uncooked shrimp (26-30 per lb.),
  peeled and deveined
  Oil for deep-fat frying
  Sweet chili sauce, optional

1. In a large bowl, combine the first
4 ingredients. Stir in cold club soda until
combined; mixture will be lumpy. Using
a paring knife, cut small slits along the
inside of the shrimp to allow it to lie flat
without curling up.
2. In an electric skillet or deep-fat fryer,
heat oil to 375°. Dip shrimp into batter,
then directly into hot oil. Fry shrimp, a
few at a time, for 1-2 minutes, or until
golden brown. Drain on paper towels.
If desired, served with sweet chili sauce.
1 shrimp: 47 cal., 2g fat (0 sat. fat), 21mg
chol., 394mg sod., 5g carb. (0 sugars,
0 fiber), 3g pro.

FISH & FRIES
INSPIRED BY: LONG JOHN SILVER'S®,
PACIFIC COD AND FRIES

Dine as though you're in a traditional
British pub. These moist fish fillets from
the oven have a fuss-free coating that's
healthy but just as crunchy and golden
as the deep-fried kind. Simply seasoned
and baked, the crispy fries are perfect
on the side.
—*Janice Mitchell, Aurora, CO*

PREP: 10 min. • **BAKE:** 35 min.
MAKES: 4 servings

- 1 lb. potatoes (about 2 medium)
- 2 Tbsp. olive oil
- ¼ tsp. pepper

FISH
- ⅓ cup all-purpose flour
- ¼ tsp. pepper
- 1 large egg
- 2 Tbsp. water
- ⅔ cup crushed cornflakes
- 1 Tbsp. grated Parmesan cheese
- ⅛ tsp. cayenne pepper
- 1 lb. haddock or cod fillets
  Tartar sauce, optional

1. Preheat oven to 425°. Peel and cut
potatoes lengthwise into ½-in.-thick
slices; cut slices into ½-in.-thick sticks.
2. In a large bowl, toss potatoes with oil
and pepper. Transfer to a 15x10x1-in.
baking pan coated with cooking spray.
Bake, uncovered, 25-30 minutes or until
golden brown and crisp, stirring once.
3. Meanwhile, in a shallow bowl, mix
flour and pepper. In another shallow
bowl, whisk egg with water. In a third
bowl, toss cornflakes with cheese and
cayenne. Dip fish in flour mixture to coat
both sides; shake off excess. Dip in egg
mixture, then in the cornflake mixture,
patting to help coating adhere.
4. Place on a baking sheet coated with
cooking spray. Bake for 10-12 minutes
or until fish just begins to flake easily
with a fork. Serve with potatoes and,
if desired, tartar sauce.
1 serving: 376 cal., 9g fat (2g sat. fat),
120mg chol., 228mg sod., 44g carb.
(3g sugars, 2g fiber), 28g pro. **Diabetic
exchanges:** 3 starch, 3 lean meat, 1½ fat.

COPYCAT CHEESECAKE
FACTORY SHRIMP SCAMPI

COPYCAT CHEESECAKE FACTORY SHRIMP SCAMPI

INSPIRED BY: CHEESECAKE FACTORY®, SHRIMP SCAMPI

Shrimp scampi is a favorite at restaurants from coast to coast. Give this half-hour copycat a try when you're craving the popular pasta dish but don't want to leave the comforts of home.
—Taste of Home *Test Kitchen*

TAKES: 30 min. • **MAKES:** 4 servings

- 12 oz. uncooked angel hair pasta
- ½ cup all-purpose flour
- 2 Tbsp. grated Parmesan cheese
- ½ tsp. salt
- ¼ tsp. pepper
- 1½ lbs. uncooked shrimp (26-30 per lb.), peeled and deveined
- 3 Tbsp. butter

SAUCE
- 2 Tbsp. olive oil
- 1 small shallot, chopped
- 5 garlic cloves
- 1 cup dry white wine
- 2 cups heavy whipping cream
- 2 plum tomatoes, diced
- 6 fresh basil leaves, thinly sliced
- 2 Tbsp. grated Parmesan cheese
- ½ tsp. salt
- ¼ tsp. pepper

1. Cook pasta according to package directions. Meanwhile, combine flour, Parmesan cheese, salt and pepper in a shallow dish. Add the shrimp; turn to coat, shaking off excess flour mixture. In a large skillet, melt the butter over medium heat; add shrimp. Cook and stir 3-5 minutes or until shrimp turn pink. Remove and keep warm.
2. In the same skillet, heat the oil over medium heat; add the shallot. Cook and stir until tender, 2-3 minutes. Add garlic cloves; cook 1 minute longer. Stir in wine. Bring to a boil. Reduce the heat; simmer, uncovered, until reduced by about half, 3-4 minutes. Stir in the cream; simmer, uncovered, until slightly thickened, about 5 minutes. Remove and discard garlic cloves. Stir in tomatoes, basil, Parmesan cheese, salt and pepper.
3. Drain pasta. To serve, spoon sauce into shallow dishes. Top with pasta and shrimp and, if desired, additional basil.
2½ cups: 1121 cal., 64g fat (36g sat. fat), 370mg chol., 993mg sod., 86g carb. (7g sugars, 4g fiber), 46g pro.

AIR-FRYER ROTISSERIE CHICKEN

AIR-FRYER ROTISSERIE CHICKEN

INSPIRED BY: BOSTON MARKET®, WHOLE CHICKEN

This air-fryer whole chicken is so crispy and yet so succulent, just like the rotisserie chickens you get at Boston Market. I serve it straight up, but you can also shred it and add it to tacos, soups, pasta salads and so much more.
—Dawn Parker, Surrey, BC

PREP: 5 min. • **COOK:** 65 min. + standing
MAKES: 6 servings

- 1 broiler/fryer chicken (3 to 4 lbs.)
- 1 Tbsp. olive oil
- 2 tsp. seasoned salt

Preheat air fryer to 350°. Brush outside of chicken with olive oil and sprinkle with seasoned salt. Place chicken, breast side down, on tray in air-fryer basket; cook 30 minutes. Flip chicken and cook until a thermometer inserted in thickest part of thigh reads 170°-175°, 35-40 minutes longer. Remove the chicken; let stand for 15 minutes before carving.

Note: In our testing, we find cook times vary dramatically between brands of air fryers. As a result, we give wider than normal ranges on suggested cook times. Begin checking at the first time listed and adjust as needed.
5 oz. cooked chicken: 313 cal., 19g fat (5g sat. fat), 104mg chol., 596mg sod., 0 carb. (0 sugars, 0 fiber), 33g pro.

COPY THAT!

Treating a chicken for the air fryer is similar to preparing a chicken for the oven. You want the least amount of moisture possible, so be sure to pat your chicken dry before seasoning. The drier the skin, then the crispier and more delicious it will be.

CASHEW CHICKEN WITH GINGER
INSPIRED BY: CHEESECAKE FACTORY®,
SPICY CASHEW CHICKEN

There are lots of recipes for cashew chicken, but my family thinks this one stands alone. We love the flavor from the fresh ginger and the crunch of the cashews. Plus, it's easy to prepare.
—*Oma Rollison, El Cajon, CA*

TAKES: 30 min. • **MAKES:** 6 servings

- 2 Tbsp. cornstarch
- 1 Tbsp. brown sugar
- 1¼ cups chicken broth
- 2 Tbsp. soy sauce
- 3 Tbsp. canola oil, divided
- 1½ lbs. boneless skinless chicken breasts, cut into 1-in. pieces
- ½ lb. sliced fresh mushrooms
- 1 small green pepper, cut into strips
- 1 can (8 oz.) sliced water chestnuts, drained
- 1½ tsp. grated fresh gingerroot
- 4 green onions, sliced
- ¾ cup salted cashews
   Hot cooked rice

1. Mix first 4 ingredients until smooth. In a large skillet, heat 2 Tbsp. oil over medium-high heat; stir-fry chicken until no longer pink. Remove from pan.
2. In same pan, heat remaining oil over medium-high heat; stir-fry mushrooms, pepper, water chestnuts and ginger until pepper is crisp-tender, 3-5 minutes. Stir broth mixture; add to pan with green onions; bring to a boil. Cook and stir until sauce is thickened, 1-2 minutes.
3. Stir in chicken and cashews; heat through. Serve with rice.

¾ cup chicken mixture: 349 cal., 19g fat (3g sat. fat), 64mg chol., 650mg sod., 18g carb. (6g sugars, 2g fiber), 28g pro. **Diabetic exchanges:** 3 lean meat, 3 fat, 1 starch.

BROILED LOBSTER TAIL

BROILED LOBSTER TAIL
INSPIRED BY: OUTBACK STEAKHOUSE®,
LOBSTER TAILS

No matter where you live, these succulent, buttery lobster tails are just a few minutes away. Here in Iowa, we use frozen lobster with delicious results, but if you're near the ocean, by all means use fresh!
—*Lauren McAnelly, Des Moines, IA*

PREP: 30 min. • **COOK:** 5 min.
MAKES: 4 servings

- 4 lobster tails (5 to 6 oz. each), thawed
- ¼ cup cold butter, cut into thin slices
   Salt and pepper to taste
   Lemon wedges

1. Preheat the broiler. Using kitchen scissors, cut a 2-in.-wide rectangle from the top shell of each lobster tail; loosen from lobster meat and remove.
2. Pull away edges of remaining shell to release lobster meat from sides; pry meat loose from bottom shell, keeping tail end attached. Place in a foil-lined 15x10x1-in. pan. Arrange butter slices over lobster meat.
3. Broil 5-6 in. from heat until meat is opaque, 5-8 minutes. Season with salt and pepper to taste; serve with lemon wedges.

Note: Recipe may be prepared using a compound herb butter instead of plain butter. To make compound butter, process ¼ cup softened butter with fresh herbs and seasonings of choice in a small food processor. Transfer mixture to a sheet of waxed paper; roll into a log, then refrigerate until firm. To use, unwrap and cut into thin slices.

1 lobster tail: 211 cal., 13g fat (8g sat. fat), 211mg chol., 691mg sod., 0 carb. (0 sugars, 0 fiber), 24g pro.

Lemon-Chive Compound Butter: Add 2 Tbsp. chopped fresh chives, 2 Tbsp. chopped fresh parsley, 1 Tbsp. minced shallot, 1 minced garlic clove, ½ tsp. grated lemon peel and ¼ tsp. salt to ¼ cup butter.

Chimichurri Compound Butter: Add 2 Tbsp. chopped fresh cilantro, 2 Tbsp. chopped fresh parsley, 1 Tbsp. minced shallot, 1 tsp. grated lemon peel, 1 tsp. minced fresh oregano, 1 minced garlic clove, ¼ tsp. salt and ⅛ tsp. crushed red pepper flakes to ¼ cup butter.

CRACKER
BARREL
MEAT LOAF

CRACKER BARREL MEAT LOAF

INSPIRED BY: CRACKER BARREL®, *MEAT LOAF*

If you've never been a fan of meat loaf, we're pretty sure this version is about to change your mind. While some meat loaves tend to be dry and not-so-tasty, this copycat entree is packed with flavor and melt-in-your-mouth goodness.
—Taste of Home *Test Kitchen*

PREP: 15 min. • **BAKE:** 1 hour + standing
MAKES: 12 servings

- 2 large eggs, beaten
- ⅓ cup 2% milk
- 1½ cups shredded cheddar cheese
- 1 sleeve crushed Ritz crackers (30 crackers)
- ½ cup finely chopped onion
- ½ cup finely chopped green pepper
- ½ tsp. salt
- ¼ tsp. garlic powder
- ¼ tsp. pepper
- 2 lbs. ground beef
- ½ cup ketchup
- 3 Tbsp. brown sugar
- 2 tsp. Dijon or yellow mustard

1. Preheat oven to 350°. In a large bowl, combine eggs, milk, cheese, crackers, onion, green pepper, salt, garlic powder and pepper. Crumble beef over mixture and mix lightly but thoroughly. Shape into a 5-in. x 10-in. loaf in an ungreased 13x9-in. baking dish. Bake, uncovered, for 50 minutes.
2. Meanwhile, in a small bowl, combine the ketchup, brown sugar and mustard. Spoon over meat loaf.
3. Bake until a thermometer reads 160°, 10-15 minutes longer. Let stand 10 minutes before slicing. If desired, sprinkle with parsley.
1 piece: 305 cal., 19g fat (8g sat. fat), 99mg chol., 504mg sod., 13g carb. (7g sugars, 0 fiber), 20g pro.

HAVE IT YOUR WAY.

If you're looking for something slightly healthier, try subbing in some ground turkey to cut down on the fat.

HOW-TO

Trade Secrets

- Combine ingredients with a spatula to prevent over mixing.
- Cook uncovered for a crispier exterior and a juicy interior,
- Both Dijon and yellow mustard work in the sauce, so feel free to use what you have on hand.
- Be generous with the sauce. Brush an even layer over top and sides.

INSPIRED BY
OLIVE GARDEN®,
FRIED LASAGNA

COPYCAT OLIVE GARDEN
FRIED LASAGNA, P. 76

POPULAR
PIZZA & PASTA

It may be tempting to phone up your favorite pizza and pasta places on a Friday night, but you can make more mouthwatering versions at home!

SPEEDY CHICKEN MARSALA

FIVE-CHEESE ZITI AL FORNO

INSPIRED BY: OLIVE GARDEN®, *FIVE-CHEESE ZITI AL FORNO*

After having the five-cheese ziti at Olive Garden, I tried to make my own homemade version—and I think I got pretty close.
—*Keri Whitney, Castro Valley, CA*

PREP: 20 min. • **BAKE:** 30 min. + standing
MAKES: 12 servings

- 1½ lbs. (about 7½ cups) uncooked ziti or small tube pasta
- 2 jars (24 oz. each) marinara sauce
- 1 jar (15 oz.) Alfredo sauce
- 2 cups shredded part-skim mozzarella cheese, divided
- ½ cup reduced-fat ricotta cheese
- ½ cup shredded provolone cheese
- ½ cup grated Romano cheese

TOPPING
- ½ cup grated Parmesan cheese
- ½ cup panko bread crumbs
- 3 garlic cloves, minced
- 2 Tbsp. olive oil
  Optional: Minced fresh parsley or basil, optional

1. Preheat oven to 350°. Cook the pasta according to the package directions for al dente; drain.
2. Meanwhile, in a large Dutch oven, combine the marinara sauce, Alfredo sauce, 1 cup mozzarella and the ricotta, provolone and Romano. Cook mixture over medium heat until sauce begins to simmer and cheeses are melted. Stir in the cooked pasta; pour mixture into a greased 13x9-in. baking dish. Top with remaining 1 cup mozzarella cheese.
3. In a small bowl, stir together the Parmesan, bread crumbs, garlic and olive oil; sprinkle over the pasta.
4. Bake, uncovered, until mixture is bubbly and topping is golden brown, 30-40 minutes. Let stand 10 minutes before serving. Garnish with fresh parsley or basil if desired.
Freeze option: Cool unbaked casserole; cover and freeze. To use, partially thaw in the refrigerator overnight. Remove from refrigerator 30 minutes before baking. Preheat oven to 350°. Cover casserole with foil; bake for 50 minutes. Uncover; bake casserole until heated through and a thermometer inserted in center reads 165°, 15-20 minutes longer.
1 cup: 449 cal., 15g fat (8g sat. fat), 32mg chol., 960mg sod., 59g carb. (11g sugars, 4g fiber), 21g pro.

SPEEDY CHICKEN MARSALA

INSPIRED BY: ROMANO'S MACARONI GRILL®, *CHICKEN MARSALA*

Since this is one of our favorite dishes to order in restaurants, I created my own version that could be made in a flash for weeknight dinners.
—*Trisha Kruse, Eagle, ID*

TAKES: 30 min. • **MAKES:** 4 servings

- 8 oz. uncooked whole wheat or multigrain angel hair pasta
- 4 boneless skinless chicken breast halves (5 oz. each)
- ¼ cup all-purpose flour
- 1 tsp. lemon-pepper seasoning
- ½ tsp. salt
- 2 Tbsp. olive oil, divided
- 4 cups sliced fresh mushrooms
- 1 garlic clove, minced
- 1 cup dry Marsala wine

1. Cook pasta according to package directions. Pound chicken with a meat mallet to ¼-in. thickness. In a large resealable bag or container, mix the flour, lemon pepper and salt. Add chicken, 1 piece at a time; close bag or container and shake to coat.
2. In a large skillet, heat 1 Tbsp. oil over medium heat. Add chicken; cook for 4-5 minutes on each side or until no longer pink. Remove from pan.
3. In the same skillet, heat remaining the 1 Tbsp. oil over medium-high heat. Add the mushrooms; cook and stir until tender. Add garlic; cook 1 minute longer. Add wine; bring to a boil. Cook until liquid is reduced by half, 5-6 minutes, stirring to loosen browned bits from pan. Return chicken to the pan, turning to coat with sauce; heat through.
4. Drain the pasta; serve with the chicken mixture.
1 serving: 493 cal., 11g fat (2g sat. fat), 78mg chol., 279mg sod., 50g carb. (4g sugars, 7g fiber), 40g pro.

WHY YOU'LL LOVE IT ...

"My family loves this dish. My daughter said that she can't order the restaurant version when dining out as it just can't compare."
—LESLIEKERNOZEK TASTEOFHOME.COM

FIVE-CHEESE
ZITI AL FORNO

COPYCAT
PASTA DA VINCI

COPYCAT PASTA DA VINCI

INSPIRED BY: CHEESECAKE FACTORY®,
PASTA DI VINCI

I fell in love with this dish at the restaurant and experimented until I could duplicate it. I think mine is just as good if not better! The sauce can be made ahead and refrigerated or frozen. Thaw if frozen and warm gently in a large skillet. Cook pasta and you have a delicious dinner on a weeknight.
—*Trisha Kruse, Eagle, ID*

PREP: 25 min. • **COOK:** 35 min.
MAKES: 8 servings

- 1   pkg. (16 oz.) penne pasta
- 1   large red onion, diced
- 2   Tbsp. olive oil
- 3   garlic cloves, minced
- 1½ lbs. boneless skinless chicken breasts, cubed
- ½   lb. sliced fresh mushrooms
- 2   cups dry white wine
- 1   can (14½ oz.) beef broth
- 1   pkg. (8 oz.) cream cheese, softened
- ½   cup butter, softened
- ½   cup half-and-half cream, room temperature
- ½   tsp. salt
- ¼   tsp. pepper
- ½   cup grated Parmesan cheese, divided
      Minced fresh parsley, optional

1. Cook pasta according to package directions for al dente. Meanwhile, in a large skillet, cook the onion in oil over medium heat until softened, 4-5 minutes. Add garlic; cook 1 minute longer. Stir in chicken and mushrooms. Cook, stirring frequently, 5-7 minutes or until the chicken is no longer pink. With a slotted spoon, remove mixture.
2. To the same skillet, add wine and broth; bring mixture to a simmer. Cook for 15-20 minutes or until the liquid is reduced by half. Reduce heat to low; add cream cheese and butter, whisking until melted. Whisk in cream, salt and pepper. Add chicken mixture to pan; heat through on low. Toss with pasta and ¼ cup Parmesan cheese. Top with remaining ¼ cup Parmesan cheese and, if desired, parsley.
1½ cups: 634 cal., 31g fat (16g sat. fat), 118mg chol., 706mg sod., 49g carb. (5g sugars, 3g fiber), 30g pro.

HOMEMADE
MEATLESS
SPAGHETTI
SAUCE

HOMEMADE MEATLESS SPAGHETTI SAUCE

INSPIRED BY: OLIVE GARDEN®,
MARINARA DIPPING SAUCE

When my tomatoes ripen, the first thing I make is this homemade spaghetti sauce.
—*Sondra Bergy, Lowell, MI*

PREP: 20 min. • **COOK:** 3¼ hours
MAKES: 2 qt.

- 4   medium onions, chopped
- ½   cup canola oil
- 12 cups chopped peeled fresh tomatoes
- 4   garlic cloves, minced
- 3   bay leaves
- 4   tsp. salt
- 2   tsp. dried oregano
- 1¼ tsp. pepper
- ½   tsp. dried basil
- 2   cans (6 oz. each) tomato paste
- ⅓   cup packed brown sugar
      Hot cooked pasta
      Minced fresh basil, optional

1. In a Dutch oven, saute onions in oil until tender. Add the tomatoes, garlic, bay leaves, salt, oregano, pepper and basil. Bring to a boil. Reduce the heat; cover and simmer mixture for 2 hours, stirring occasionally.
2. Add tomato paste and brown sugar; simmer, uncovered, for 1 hour. Discard bay leaves. Serve with the pasta and, if desired, basil.
½ cup: 133 cal., 7g fat (1g sat. fat), 0 chol., 614mg sod., 17g carb. (12g sugars, 3g fiber), 2g pro.

HAVE IT YOUR WAY.

Browned ground beef or Italian sausage can be added to the cooked sauce if desired.

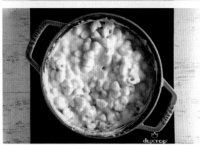

**COPYCAT
MAC & CHEESE**

Make the Best Mac

- Cubing the butter helps it melt evenly and quickly.
- A roux of flour and fat (butter) is the secret to this dish.
- Stir the cheese into the cream sauce until it's well melted.
- Make sure the pasta is completely covered with the cream sauce before serving.

COPYCAT MAC & CHEESE

INSPIRED BY: PANERA BREAD®, *MAC & CHEESE*
My kids and I love mac and cheese. We always get it in the bread bowls when we're at Panera, but with three cheeses, these white cheddar shells are filling on their own.
—*Steven Schend, Grand Rapids, MI*

TAKES: 25 min. • **MAKES:** 6 servings

3½   cups uncooked pipetti pasta, such as Barilla Pippetti, or medium pasta shells
¼   cup butter, cubed
¼   cup all-purpose flour
2½   cups 2% milk
¼   tsp. pepper
2   cups shredded white cheddar cheese
4   slices white American cheese, chopped
¼   cup grated Parmesan cheese
     Bread bowls, optional

Cook the pasta according to package directions; drain and set aside. In a large saucepan, melt butter over low heat; whisk in flour until smooth. Whisk in milk and pepper. Bring to a boil; cook and stir 2 minutes or until thickened. Stir in cheeses until melted; stir in pasta. Serve in bread bowls if desired.
1 cup: 538 cal., 27g fat (16g sat. fat), 79mg chol., 565mg sod., 50g carb. (7g sugars, 2g fiber), 23g pro.

COPY THAT!

When it comes to getting the smoothest cheese sauce possible, it's best to shred the cheese yourself. If you use store-bought shredded cheese, you may find your sauce has a little grittiness to it and the cheese may not melt completely. That's because some shredded cheeses contain cellulose, which helps cheese from clumping together in the bag. It's going to be worth the extra effort to shred the cheese yourself. You can make it a little easier by using a food processor with the grater attachment.

PRETZEL CRUST PIZZA

PRETZEL CRUST PIZZA

INSPIRED BY: LITTLE CAESARS®,
PRETZEL CRUST

In our house, we love pizza and pretzel bread! When Little Caesar's came out with their pretzel crust pizza, we fell in love but also knew it was unrealistic to be buying it all the time. The next best thing was to make it ourselves, and it came out even better than the restaurant's version! This thick-crusted copycat pizza is bound to blow your socks off! Hope you enjoy!
—*Mary Lou Timpson, Centennial Park, AZ*

PREP: 25 in. + rising
BAKE: 20 min. • **MAKES:** 8 servings

- 1½ **cups warm water (110° to 115°)**
- 2 **Tbsp. sugar**
- 1 **Tbsp. active dry yeast**
- 4 **cups all-purpose flour**
- 1 **tsp. salt**
- ½ **cup hot water**
- 2 **Tbsp. baking soda**
- ¼ **tsp. pretzel or coarse salt**
PIZZA
- ½ **cup salsa con queso dip, such as Tostitos**
- 2 **cups shredded Mexican cheese blend**
- ½ **cup sliced pepperoni**
- 1 **Tbsp. butter, melted**

1. In a stand mixer, stir together warm water, sugar and yeast; let stand until foamy, 4-5 minutes. Add flour and 1 tsp. table salt. Using a dough hook, mix on low speed until dough comes together, 1-2 minutes. Increase speed to medium and mix an additional 5 minutes. Place dough in a greased bowl, turning once to grease the top. Cover and let dough rise in a warm place until doubled, about 45 minutes.
2. Preheat oven to 425°. Punch down dough; press into a 12-in. circle onto an ungreased 14-in. pizza pan. Let stand 10 minutes. Stir together hot water and baking soda; brush mixture over outer 1-in. Let stand for 5 minutes; repeat. Sprinkle coarse salt over the edge.
3. Spread queso dip over inside of crust. Top with the cheese and pepperoni. Bake until crust is golden brown and cheese is melted, 16-18 minutes. Brush crust with melted butter before serving.
1 piece: 414 cal., 15g fat (7g sat. fat), 36mg chol., 772mg sod., 55g carb. (4g sugars, 3g fiber), 15g pro.

HOMEMADE FETTUCCINE ALFREDO

INSPIRED BY: OLIVE GARDEN®,
ALFREDO SAUCE

This easy Alfredo sauce is creamy and comforting, and it coats fettuccine noodles in fine fashion. It tastes surprisingly close to the Olive Garden's Alfredo, but just a little better.
—*Jo Gray, Park City, MT*

TAKES: 20 min. • **MAKES:** 2 servings

- 4 **oz. uncooked fettuccine**
- 3 **Tbsp. butter**
- 1 **cup heavy whipping cream**
- ¼ **cup plus 2 Tbsp. grated Parmesan cheese, divided**
- ¼ **cup grated Romano cheese**
- 1 **large egg yolk, lightly beaten**
- ⅛ **tsp. salt**
Dash each pepper and ground nutmeg
Minced fresh parsley, optional

Cook fettuccine according to package directions. Meanwhile, in a saucepan, melt butter over medium-low heat. Stir in cream, ¼ cup Parmesan cheese, Romano cheese, egg yolk, salt, pepper and nutmeg. Cook and stir over medium-low heat until a thermometer reads 160° (do not boil). Drain the fettuccine; combine with the Alfredo sauce and remaining 2 Tbsp. Parmesan cheese. If desired, sprinkle with parsley.
1 cup: 907 cal., 73g fat (45g sat. fat), 290mg chol., 835mg sod., 45g carb. (5g sugars, 2g fiber), 23g pro.

**BLUSHING
PENNE PASTA**

BLUSHING PENNE PASTA

INSPIRED BY: NOODLES & COMPANY®,
PENNE ROSA

I reworked this recipe from an original
that called for vodka and heavy whipping
cream. My friends and family had a hard
time believing a sauce this rich, flavorful
and creamy could be light.
—*Margaret Wilson, San Bernardino, CA*

TAKES: 30 min. • **MAKES:** 8 servings

- 1   pkg. (16 oz.) penne pasta
- 2   Tbsp. butter
- 1   medium onion, halved and
      thinly sliced
- 2   Tbsp. minced fresh thyme or
      2 tsp. dried thyme
- 2   Tbsp. minced fresh basil or
      2 tsp. dried basil
- 1   tsp. salt
- 1½ cups half-and-half cream, divided
- ½   cup white wine or reduced-sodium
      chicken broth
- 1   Tbsp. tomato paste
- 2   Tbsp. all-purpose flour
- ½   cup shredded Parmigiano-
      Reggiano cheese, divided

1. In a 6-qt. stockpot, cook penne pasta
according to package directions. Drain;
return to pot.
2. Meanwhile, in a large nonstick skillet,
heat butter over medium heat; saute
onion for 8-10 minutes or until lightly
browned. Add herbs and salt; cook and
stir 1 minute. Add 1 cup cream, wine and
tomato paste; cook and stir until blended.
3. Mix flour and remaining ½ cup cream
until smooth; gradually stir into the onion
mixture. Bring to a boil; cook and stir
until thickened, about 2 minutes. Stir
in ¼ cup cheese. Stir into pasta. Serve
with remaining ¼ cup cheese.
1 cup: 335 cal., 10g fat (6g sat. fat), 34mg
chol., 431mg sod., 47g carb. (4g sugars,
2g fiber), 12g pro.

WHY YOU'LL LOVE IT ...

*"This was such a breeze to make and
tastes great! I really liked the strong
spice blend with the light sauce.
Even tastes great as leftovers!"*
—LPHJKITCHEN, TASTEOFHOME.COM

COPYCAT OLIVE GARDEN FRIED LASAGNA

INSPIRED BY: OLIVE GARDEN®,
FRIED LASAGNA

One of my favorite dishes at Olive Garden
is their fried lasagna. On a whim, I tried
to re-create it at home. After a few tries,
I think I got it pretty close to the original.
—*Jolene Martinelli, Fremont, NH*

PREP: 45 min. + freezing
COOK: 10 min./batch
MAKES: 10 servings

- 20   uncooked lasagna noodles
- 1   carton (32 oz.) whole-milk
       ricotta cheese
- 2½   cups shredded Italian cheese
       blend, divided
- 2   cups shredded part-skim
       mozzarella cheese
- 6   large eggs, beaten, divided use
- 4   tsp. Italian seasoning, divided
       Oil for deep-fat frying
- 2½   cups panko bread crumbs
- 1   jar (24 oz.) marinara sauce,
       warmed
- 1   jar (15 oz.) Alfredo sauce, warmed

1. Cook lasagna noodles according to
package directions for al dente. In a
large bowl, combine ricotta, 1¼ cups
Italian cheese blend, mozzarella, 2 eggs
and 3 tsp. Italian seasoning. Drain the
noodles. If desired, cut off ribboned
edges (discard or save for another use).
Spread about ¼ cup filling on each
noodle. Starting with a short side, fold
each in thirds. Place all on a parchment-
lined baking sheet, seam side down.
Freeze just until firm, about 1 hour.
2. In an electric skillet or deep fryer, heat
oil to 375°. In a shallow bowl, mix bread
crumbs, ⅔ cup Italian cheese blend and
remaining 1 tsp. Italian seasoning. Place
remaining 4 eggs in a separate shallow
bowl. Dip the lasagna bundles into eggs,
then into the crumb mixture, patting to
help crumb coating adhere.
3. Fry bundles in batches until golden
brown, 8-10 minutes, turning once. Drain
on paper towels. Serve fried lasagna
with marinara, Alfredo, the remaining
Italian cheese blend and, if desired,
additional Italian seasoning.
2 lasagna rolls: 876 cal., 54g fat (19g sat.
fat), 195mg chol., 1011mg sod., 61g carb.
(11g sugars, 4g fiber), 37g pro.

COPYCAT OLIVE GARDEN
FRIED LASAGNA

PASTA
NAPOLITANA

PASTA NAPOLITANA

INSPIRED BY: OLIVE GARDEN®, *MEAT SAUCE*

This is the ultimate meat lover's pasta and is my copycat version of the Olive Garden's version. Rich and hearty, with tremendous flavors, this dish will disappear quickly. I always make extra sauce, as it freezes very well.

—John Pittman, Northampton, PA

PREP: 30 min. • **COOK:** 2 hours
MAKES: 8 servings

- 8   bacon strips
- 1   lb. ground beef
- 1   lb. bulk Italian sausage
- 1   Tbsp. olive oil
- 1   large onion, chopped
- 1   can (6 oz.) tomato paste
- 1   jar (24 oz.) marinara sauce
- 1   can (14½ oz.) chicken broth
- ½   cup dry red wine
- 1   can (8 oz.) mushroom stems and pieces
- ⅓   cup pepperoni, chopped
- 1   Tbsp. sugar
- 1   Tbsp. garlic powder
- 1   Tbsp. dried oregano
- 1   Tbsp. dried basil
- 2   tsp. dried parsley flakes
- 1   tsp. dried rosemary, crushed
- 1   tsp. dried marjoram
- 1   tsp. rubbed sage
- 1   tsp. seasoned salt
- 1   tsp. pepper
- ½   to 1 tsp. crushed red pepper flakes
- 1   tsp. Worcestershire sauce
      Hot cooked spaghetti
      Grated Parmesan cheese

1. In a Dutch oven, cook bacon over medium heat; drain and set aside. Discard drippings. In same pan, cook ground beef and sausage in olive oil until beef is no longer pink, breaking meat into crumbles. Add onion; cook until tender, about 5 minutes. Drain. Add tomato paste; cook and stir until fragrant, about 5 minutes.
2. Stir in bacon, marinara sauce, broth, wine, mushrooms, pepperoni, sugar, garlic powder, oregano, basil, parsley, rosemary, marjoram, sage, seasoned salt, pepper, pepper flakes and the Worcestershire sauce. Bring to a boil; reduce heat. Simmer, covered, stirring occasionally, until thickened and flavors have combined, about 2 hours. Serve with spaghetti and Parmesan cheese.
1 serving: 427 cal., 28g fat (9g sat. fat), 82mg chol., 1591mg sod., 19g carb. (10g sugars, 4g fiber), 24g pro.

CALIFORNIA CHICKEN CLUB PIZZA

CALIFORNIA CHICKEN CLUB PIZZA

INSPIRED BY: CALIFORNIA PIZZA KITCHEN®, *CALIFORNIA CLUB PIZZA*

Inspired by the California Club pizza from California Pizza Kitchen, I decided to whip up my own version. It's loaded with tons of fresh veggies, so that means it has to be good for you, right?

—Robert Pickart, Chicago, IL

PREP: 25 min. • **BAKE:** 10 min.
MAKES: 4 servings

- 1   Tbsp. cornmeal
- 1   loaf (1 lb.) frozen pizza dough, thawed
- 1   cup shredded mozzarella cheese
- 1   cup ready-to-use grilled chicken breast strips
- 4   bacon strips, cooked and crumbled
- 2   cups shredded romaine
- 1   cup fresh arugula
- ¼   cup mayonnaise
- 1   Tbsp. lemon juice
- 1   tsp. grated lemon zest
- ½   tsp. pepper
- 1   medium tomato, thinly sliced
- 1   medium ripe avocado, peeled and sliced
- ¼   cup loosely packed basil leaves, chopped

1. Preheat oven to 450°. Grease a 14-in. pizza pan; sprinkle with cornmeal. On a floured surface, roll dough into a 13-in. circle. Transfer to prepared pan; build up edges slightly. Sprinkle with cheese, chicken and bacon. Bake until crust is lightly browned, 10-12 minutes.
2. Meanwhile, place romaine and arugula in a large bowl. In a small bowl, combine mayonnaise, lemon juice, lemon zest and pepper. Pour over lettuces; toss to coat. Arrange lettuce over warm pizza. Top with tomato, avocado and basil. Serve pizza immediately.
2 slices: 612 cal., 30g fat (7g sat. fat), 51mg chol., 859mg sod., 59g carb. (4g sugars, 5g fiber), 29g pro.

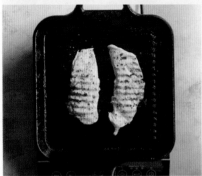

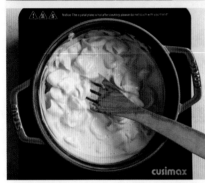

ASIAGO TORTELLONI ALFREDO WITH GRILLED CHICKEN

ASIAGO TORTELLINI ALFREDO WITH GRILLED CHICKEN

INSPIRED BY: OLIVE GARDEN®, *ASIAGO TORTELLONI ALFREDO WITH GRILLED CHICKEN*

My family loves all types of pasta but this one is one of their favorites. Swap in your favorite flavor of tortellini if you can't find any with Asiago.
—*Susan Hein, Burlington, WI*

TAKES: 30 min. • **MAKES:** 4 servings

- 4 boneless skinless chicken breasts (6 oz. each)
- 1 Tbsp. olive oil
- ½ tsp. salt
- ¼ tsp. pepper
- 1 pkg. (9 oz.) refrigerated cheese tortellini
- 1 jar (15 oz.) Alfredo sauce, warmed
- ½ cup grated Asiago cheese

1. Pound chicken breasts with a meat mallet to ½-in. thickness. Brush with oil and sprinkle with salt and pepper. Place chicken on oiled grill rack. Grill, covered, over medium heat until a thermometer reads 165°, 4-5 minutes on each side.

2. Meanwhile, cook tortellini according to package directions. Preheat broiler. Drain tortellini and toss with hot Alfredo sauce. Transfer to a greased broiler-safe 9-in. square baking dish; sprinkle with Asiago. Broil 3-4 in. from heat until top is golden brown, 2-3 minutes.

3. To serve, slice chicken and place on top of tortellini. Sprinkle with additional Asiago if desired.

1 chicken breast half with 1 cup pasta: 543 cal., 24g fat (12g sat. fat), 153mg chol., 1161mg sod., 31g carb. (1g sugars, 2g fiber), 48g pro.

HOW-TO

Make It Your Own with These Tips

- A silicone brush works best for brushing on the oil.
- Don't feel like grilling? Broil chicken in the oven or saute on the stovetop in a skillet.
- If you don't like jarred Alfredo sauce, feel free to use your own recipe.
- We sprinkled on more Asiago before broiling, but you can add Parmesan or a cheese blend.

HAVE IT YOUR WAY.

If you find yourself without a grill or a grill pan, you could always cook the chicken in a skillet. Heat up a cast-iron or nonstick skillet with some butter or olive oil, and cook the chicken as you would in a grill pan. Use a thermometer to ensure the chicken is sufficiently cooked and hits 165°.

ITALIAN MEAT STROMBOLI

CHEESY BREAD
INSPIRED BY: DOMINO'S®, *CHEESY BREAD*
Get Domino's cheesy bread right from your own oven! Using refrigerated French bread dough makes it easy to get restaurant-style bread in just minutes.
—Taste of Home *Test Kitchen*

PREP: 20 min. • **BAKE:** 20 min.
MAKES: 8 servings

- 1 tube (11 oz.) refrigerated crusty French loaf
- 2 cups shredded part-skim mozzarella cheese, divided
- 2 cups shredded cheddar cheese, divided
- 2 Tbsp. butter, melted
- ¼ cup shredded Romano cheese
- 2 tsp. dried parsley flakes
- ½ tsp. garlic powder
  Optional: Marinara sauce, garlic butter, ranch dressing or blue cheese dressing

1. Preheat oven to 350°. Unroll dough and pat into a 14x12-in. rectangle. Sprinkle 1¾ cups each mozzarella and cheddar lengthwise down the center of the dough. Bring edges of dough to the center over filling; pinch seam to seal.
2. Place seam side down on a greased baking sheet. Brush top with butter. In a small bowl, combine Romano, parsley, garlic powder and remaining ¼ cup each mozzarella and cheddar; sprinkle over top. Bake 20-25 minutes or until golden brown. Serve warm with dipping sauce if desired.
1 piece: 327 cal., 20g fat (11g sat. fat), 56mg chol., 631mg sod., 21g carb. (2g sugars, 0 fiber), 17g pro.

ITALIAN MEAT STROMBOLI
INSPIRED BY: SBARRO®, *PEPPERONI STROMBOLI*
As a mother of two, I seem to have time for creativity only when I'm in the kitchen. I love getting the Pepperoni Stromboli from Sbarro's, so I made my own version with ham.
—Denise Tutton, Ridgway, PA

PREP: 25 min. + rising
BAKE: 25 min. • **MAKES:** 10 servings

- 1 loaf (1 lb.) frozen bread dough, thawed
- 1 can (8 oz.) pizza sauce
- ¼ tsp. garlic powder, divided
- ¼ tsp. dried oregano, divided
- 8 oz. brick cheese, sliced
- 1 cup shredded part-skim mozzarella cheese
- ½ cup chopped green pepper
- ¼ cup chopped onion
- 1 cup sliced fresh mushrooms
- ½ cup shredded Parmesan cheese
- 1 pkg. (3 oz.) sliced pepperoni
- 5 oz. sliced deli ham

1. Place the dough in a greased bowl, turning once to grease the top. Cover and let dough rise in a warm place until doubled, about 1 hour.
2. Preheat oven to 350°. Mix the pizza sauce and ⅛ tsp. each garlic powder and oregano.
3. Punch down dough. On a lightly floured surface, roll dough into a 15x10-in. rectangle. Top with brick cheese, sauce mixture and remaining ingredients to within 1 in. of edges.
4. Roll up, jelly-roll style, starting with a long side. Pinch seam to seal and tuck ends under; transfer to a greased baking sheet. Sprinkle with the remaining ⅛ tsp. each garlic powder and oregano. Bake until golden brown, 25-30 minutes.
1 slice: 335 cal., 16g fat (8g sat. fat), 46mg chol., 871mg sod., 27g carb. (4g sugars, 3g fiber), 19g pro.

INSPIRED BY
THE WIZARDING WORLD OF
HARRY POTTER™ UNIVERSAL
ORLANDO RESORT®, *BUTTERBEER*

BUTTERBEER, P. 91

FAVORITE
ODDS & ENDS

Round out any meal with all the familiar sauces, sips and sides you no longer have to leave home for.

DOWN-HOME HUSH PUPPIES
INSPIRED BY: LONG JOHN SILVER'S®, *HUSH PUPPIES*

Hush puppies are a classic southern side. The sweet-spicy flavor of these fried bites has delighted friends and family for decades.
—*Gene Pitts, Wilsonville, AL*

PREP: 15 min. + standing
COOK: 20 min. • **MAKES:** 2½ dozen

- 1 cup cornmeal
- 1 cup self-rising flour
- 1½ tsp. baking powder
- ½ tsp. salt
- 1 large onion, chopped
- 2 jalapeno peppers, seeded and diced
- ¼ cup sugar
- 1 large egg
- 1 cup buttermilk
  Canola oil

1. In a large bowl, combine the first 7 ingredients. Add egg and buttermilk; stir just until moistened. Set aside at room temperature for 30 minutes. Do not stir again.
2. In an electric skillet or deep fryer, heat 2-3 in. oil to 375°. Drop batter by rounded tablespoonfuls, a few at a time, into hot oil. Fry until golden brown, about 1½ minutes on each side. Drain on paper towels.
Note: As a substitute for 1 cup self-rising flour, place 1½ tsp. baking powder and ½ tsp. salt in a measuring cup. Add all-purpose flour to measure 1 cup.
1 hush puppy: 73 cal., 3g fat (0 sat. fat), 7mg chol., 132mg sod., 10g carb. (2g sugars, 0 fiber), 1g pro.

JAPANESE MAYONNAISE
INSPIRED BY: KEWPIE®, *MAYONNAISE*

A few years ago, Kewpie, a Japanese mayonnaise, took America by storm. Everyone was clamoring to find a jar of it to try. It's still a little difficult to get your hands on some, so we tried to make our own version.
—*Taste of Home Test Kitchen*

TAKES: 25 min. • **MAKES:** 1¼ cups

- 2 large egg yolks
- 2 Tbsp. water, divided
- 2 tsp. lemon juice
- 2 tsp. Dijon mustard
- 1 Tbsp. sugar
- ½ tsp. dashi powder
- 1 cup canola, grapeseed or vegetable oil
- 2 Tbsp. rice vinegar

1. In a double boiler or heatproof bowl over simmering water, constantly whisk the egg yolks, 1 Tbsp. water and lemon juice until the mixture reaches 160°, 30-40 seconds. While whisking, quickly place bottom of pan or heatproof bowl in a bowl of ice water; continue whisking until cooled, 1-2 minutes.
2. Transfer to a 2-cup glass measuring cup or other narrow container. Add the mustard, sugar and dashi powder. With an immersion blender, process mixture while gradually adding the oil in a steady stream. Whisk in vinegar; if desired, add the remaining 1 Tbsp. water. Cover and refrigerate for up to 7 days.
1 Tbsp.: 110 cal., 12g fat (1g sat. fat), 18mg chol., 96mg sod., 1g carb. (1g sugars, 0 fiber), 0 pro.

SOUR CREAM & CHEDDAR BISCUITS
INSPIRED BY: RED LOBSTER®, *CHEDDAR BAY BISCUITS*

Here's my go-to recipe for biscuits. Brushing them with the garlic-butter topping before baking seals the deal!
—*Amy Martin, Vancouver, WA*

PREP: 25 min. • **BAKE:** 15 min.
MAKES: 1½ dozen

- 2½ cups all-purpose flour
- 3 tsp. baking powder
- 2 tsp. sugar
- 1 tsp. garlic powder
- ½ tsp. cream of tartar
- ¼ tsp. salt
- ¼ tsp. cayenne pepper
- ½ cup cold butter, cubed
- 1½ cups shredded cheddar cheese
- ¾ cup 2% milk
- ½ cup sour cream

TOPPING
- 6 Tbsp. butter, melted
- 1½ tsp. garlic powder
- 1 tsp. minced fresh parsley

1. Preheat oven to 450°. In a large bowl, whisk the first 7 ingredients. Cut in cold butter until mixture resembles coarse crumbs; stir in cheese. Add milk and sour cream; stir just until moistened.
2. Drop by ¼ cupfuls 2 in. apart onto greased baking sheets. Mix the topping ingredients; brush over tops. Bake until light brown, 12-15 minutes. Serve warm.
1 biscuit: 206 cal., 14g fat (8g sat. fat), 36mg chol., 256mg sod., 15g carb. (2g sugars, 1g fiber), 5g pro.

FROZEN STRAWBERRY DAIQUIRIS

FROZEN STRAWBERRY DAIQUIRIS

INSPIRED BY: CARNIVAL CRUISE LINES®, STRAWBERRY DAIQUIRIS

When I was in my early 20s, I went on a Carnival Cruise to the Caribbean. I got hooked on the frozen strawberry daiquiris and needed to come up with my own version. I think this is pretty darned close!

—*James Schend, Pleasant Prairie, WI*

TAKES: 10 min. • **MAKES:** 5 servings

- 1¼ cups rum
- ¾ cup frozen limeade concentrate, thawed
- 1 pkg. (15½ oz.) frozen sweetened sliced strawberries
- 2 to 2½ cups ice cubes
  Optional: Fresh strawberries and lime slices

In a blender, combine the rum, limeade concentrate, strawberries and ice. Cover and process until smooth and thickened (use more ice for thicker daiquiris). Pour into cocktail glasses. If desired, garnish with fresh strawberries and lime slices.
1 cup: 299 cal., 0 fat (0 sat. fat), 0 chol., 7mg sod., 45g carb. (41g sugars, 2g fiber), 1g pro.

COPY THAT!

If you don't have frozen strawberries, you can definitely use fresh ones instead. Fresh might make a frozen strawberry daiquiri slightly thinner, but you can always add more ice to balance it out. Otherwise, try using half frozen strawberries and half fresh, and settle on a ratio that creates your ideal daiquiri.

COPYCAT 57 SAUCE

INSPIRED BY: HEINZ®, *57 SAUCE*

This is a homemade version of our favorite steak sauce. We use it on steaks, chicken, pork and burgers, or as a dip for our fries. It's also great for basting grilled chicken or for barbecue ribs. You could even add it to a marinade.

—*Erin Wright, Wallace, KS*

TAKES: 20 min. • **MAKES:** 1½ cups

- ½ cup boiling water
- ½ cup raisins
- ⅔ cup ketchup
- ½ cup unsweetened applesauce
- 3 Tbsp. white vinegar
- 1 Tbsp. ground mustard
- 1 tsp. garlic powder
- 1 tsp. seasoned salt
- 1 tsp. chili powder
- 1 tsp. Worcestershire sauce
- 1 tsp. prepared yellow mustard

Pour boiling water over raisins in a small bowl; let stand 5 minutes. Drain. Transfer to a blender; add remaining ingredients. Cover and process until smooth. Strain if desired. Store in an airtight container in the refrigerator.
2 Tbsp.: 42 cal., 0 fat (0 sat. fat), 0 chol., 312mg sod., 10g carb. (8g sugars, 1g fiber), 1g pro.

SWEET POTATO CASSEROLE

GRILLED CHICKEN MARGHERITA

INSPIRED BY: OLIVE GARDEN®,
CHICKEN MARGHERITA

I've been making this dish for years, and when I saw the same dish on the menu at Olive Garden, I knew I had a winner. Fresh basil gets all the respect in this super supper—even forks will stand at attention when it hits the table.

—Judy Armstrong, Prairieville, LA

PREP: 25 min. + marinating
GRILL: 10 min. • **MAKES:** 4 servings

- 4   boneless skinless chicken breast halves (6 oz. each)
- ½   cup reduced-fat balsamic vinaigrette
- 3   garlic cloves, minced
- ½   tsp. salt
- ¼   tsp. pepper
- ¼   cup marinara sauce
- 16 fresh basil leaves
- 2   plum tomatoes, thinly sliced lengthwise
- 1   cup frozen artichoke hearts, thawed and chopped
- 3   green onions, chopped
- ¼   cup shredded part-skim mozzarella cheese

1. Flatten chicken to ½-in. thickness. In a large bowl, combine vinaigrette and garlic. Add chicken; turn to coat. Cover; refrigerate 30 minutes. Drain chicken, discarding marinade. Sprinkle chicken with salt and pepper.

2. On a lightly greased grill rack, grill chicken, covered, over medium heat or broil 4 in. from heat for 5 minutes. Turn the chicken; top with marinara, basil, tomatoes, artichokes, onions and cheese. Cover and cook until the chicken is no longer pink and cheese is melted, 5-6 minutes.

1 chicken breast: 273 cal., 8g fat (2g sat. fat), 98mg chol., 606mg sod., 10g carb. (4g sugars, 3g fiber), 38g pro. **Diabetic exchanges:** 5 lean meat, 1 vegetable, ½ fat.

WHY YOU'LL LOVE IT...

"Wow. Fast, easy, healthy and delicious! This will no doubt become a go-to recipe for us."
—CHRISSYANNE, TASTEOFHOME.COM

SWEET POTATO CASSEROLE

INSPIRED BY: BOSTON MARKET®,
SWEET POTATO CASSEROLE

I make this classic for Thanksgiving, but I also have been known to serve it with meat loaf and even grilled meat.
—Eleanor Sherry, Highland Park, IL

PREP: 10 min. • **BAKE:** 25 min.
MAKES: 8 servings

CASSEROLE
- 2¼ to 2½ lbs. sweet potatoes, cooked, peeled and mashed (about 4 cups)
- ⅓   cup butter, melted
- 2   large eggs, lightly beaten
- ½   cup 2% milk
- 1   tsp. vanilla extract
- ½   cup sugar

TOPPING
- ½   cup chopped nuts
- ½   cup sweetened shredded coconut
- ½   cup packed brown sugar
- 3   Tbsp. butter, melted

1. In a large bowl, combine mashed potatoes, butter, eggs, milk, vanilla and sugar. Spread into a greased 1½-qt. casserole dish.

2. Combine topping ingredients and sprinkle over potatoes. Bake at 375° until a thermometer reads 160°, about 25 minutes.

¾ cup: 445 cal., 21g fat (10g sat. fat), 80mg chol., 152mg sod., 62g carb. (42g sugars, 5g fiber), 6g pro.

GRILLED CHICKEN
MARGHERITA

DOLE WHIP

INSPIRED BY: DISNEYLAND THEME PARK®,
DOLE WHIP

Your kitchen will be the happiest place on earth when you serve this sweet-sour treat. The recipe comes directly from Disneyland and tastes just like the real deal you'd order at the park.
—Taste of Home *Test Kitchen*

TAKES: 10 min. • **MAKES:** 2 servings

- 2 cups frozen pineapple chunks
- 1 cup vanilla ice cream
- ½ cup unsweetened pineapple juice

Place all ingredients in a blender; cover and process until thick, stopping and scraping the sides as needed. Pipe into 2 glasses or dishes, topping with a swirl.
1 cup: 290 cal., 7g fat (4g sat. fat), 29mg chol., 87mg sod., 50g carb. (34g sugars, 1g fiber), 3g pro.

HAVE IT YOUR WAY.

You can make your creation into a float by pouring more pineapple juice over the whip. Or try loading it up with some fun toppings such as pineapple chunks, vanilla sprinkles, chocolate chips or candy pieces, or granola or nuts.

HOMEMADE
CHEEZ-ITS

HOMEMADE CHEEZ-ITS

INSPIRED BY: CHEEZ-IT®,
BAKED SNACK CRACKERS

Bring some childhood magic back to your kitchen with this homemade Cheez-Its recipe. It's a fun and delicious weekend baking project that the whole family can enjoy (and subsequently devour).
—*Lauren Habermehl, Pewaukee, WI*

PREP: 30 min. + chilling
BAKE: 15 min./batch + cooling
MAKES: 12 dozen

- 8 oz. cheddar cheese, cubed
- 1 cup all-purpose flour
- 1 tsp. cornstarch
- 1 tsp. kosher salt
- ½ tsp. ground mustard
- ½ tsp. paprika
- 4 Tbsp. cold unsalted butter
- 2 Tbsp. ice water
- 1 large egg, beaten
  Flaky sea salt, optional

1. In a food processor, pulse cheese until finely chopped; transfer to a large bowl. Stir in flour, cornstarch, salt, mustard and paprika. Cut in butter until mixture resembles coarse crumbs. Gradually add ice water, tossing with a fork until dough holds together when pressed. Shape into a disk; wrap and refrigerate 1 hour or overnight.
2. Preheat oven to 350°. On a lightly floured surface, roll dough to ⅛-in. thickness. Using a fluted pastry wheel, pizza cutter or sharp knife, cut the dough into 1-in. squares. Transfer to parchment-lined baking sheets. Using a toothpick or skewer, poke a hole in center of each square. Brush with the beaten egg; sprinkle with salt if desired.
3. Bake until crisp and lightly golden around edges, 15-18 minutes. Cool completely on baking sheets.
1 cracker: 13 cal., 1g fat (1g sat. fat), 2mg chol., 24mg sod., 1g carb. (0 sugars, 0 fiber), 0 pro.

RIB SHACK COPYCAT MASHED POTATOES

INSPIRED BY: RIB SHACK®, *MASHED POTATOES*

Idaho is known as the potato state—even our license plates say "Famous Potatoes"! This is my version of the smashers that are served at a local barbecue joint. Everyone who tries them there begs for the recipe, which the place won't give out—so I made my own copycat version.

—*Trisha Kruse, Eagle, ID*

TAKES: 30 min. • **MAKES:** 12 servings

- 2½ lbs. potatoes, peeled and cubed
- 1 cup 2% milk, warmed
- ½ cup spreadable garlic and herb cream cheese
- 3 Tbsp. butter, softened
- 1 lb. bacon strips, cooked and crumbled
- 1 cup shredded cheddar cheese
- ½ cup shredded Parmesan cheese
- 3 green onions, chopped
- 2 Tbsp. minced fresh parsley or 2 tsp. dried parsley flakes
- ¼ tsp. salt
- ¼ tsp. pepper

Place potatoes in a Dutch oven; add water to cover. Bring to a boil. Reduce heat; cook, uncovered, until tender, 15-20 minutes. Drain and return to pan; gently mash the potatoes while gradually adding milk, cream cheese and butter to reach desired consistency. Stir in remaining ingredients.

⅔ cup: 238 cal., 15g fat (8g sat. fat), 41mg chol., 477mg sod., 15g carb. (2g sugars, 1g fiber), 10g pro.

AVOCADO LIME RANCH DRESSING

INSPIRED BY: CHICK-FIL-A®, *AVOCADO LIME RANCH DRESSING*

This dressing is a Chick-fil-A copycat recipe. It has no sugar added, is half the calories of the original, and is made with buttermilk, avocado, fresh cilantro, spices and lime for a tangy, zesty twist on a classic salad dressing. Dairy-based salad dressings will last in the refrigerator for up to a week. Using freshly opened sour cream and buttermilk will help it last as long as possible.

—*Kelsey Reddick Smith, Knoxville, TN*

PREP: 15 min. + chilling • **MAKES:** 2 cups

- ½ cup buttermilk
- ½ cup sour cream
- ¼ cup mayonnaise
- 1 medium ripe avocado, peeled and cubed
- 2 Tbsp. chopped fresh cilantro
- 2 Tbsp. lime juice
- 1½ tsp. dill weed
- ½ tsp. salt
- ½ tsp. garlic powder
- ½ tsp. ground cumin
- ¼ tsp. pepper

Place all ingredients in a blender; cover and process until combined. Transfer to a jar. Refrigerate, covered, at least 1 hour before serving.

2 Tbsp.: 56 cal., 5g fat (1g sat. fat), 7mg chol., 109mg sod., 2g carb. (1g sugars, 1g fiber), 1g pro. **Diabetic exchanges:** 1 fat.

COPYCAT BURGER KING ONION RINGS

INSPIRED BY: BURGER KING®, *ONION RINGS*

Burger King onion rings are satisfying in a way that french fries can't be—it's the texture. The crunch and flavor lift your brain to some sort of euphoria. Fortunately, it's possible to make a spot-on version of Burger King onion rings at home. The King will be so proud.

—*Elizabeth King, Duluth, MN*

PREP: 20 min. • **COOK:** 5 min./batch
MAKES: 4 servings

- 1 large onion
- 1 cup all-purpose flour
- 1 tsp. baking powder
- 1 tsp. kosher salt
- 1 tsp. seasoned salt
- 1 large egg
- ½ cup whole milk
- 2 cups panko bread crumbs
- Oil for deep-fat frying

1. Cut onion into ¼-in. slices; separate into rings. In a shallow bowl, combine flour, baking powder, salt and seasoned salt. In another shallow bowl, whisk egg and milk. Place bread crumbs in a third shallow bowl. Coat onion rings with flour mixture, then dip into egg mixture, then dip into flour mixture and egg mixture again. Coat with bread crumbs, pressing to adhere.

2. In an electric skillet or deep fryer, heat oil to 375°. Fry the onion rings, a few at a time, for 30 seconds on each side or until golden brown. Drain on paper towels. Sprinkle with additional seasoned salt.

1 serving: 158 cal., 8g fat (1g sat. fat), 33mg chol., 316mg sod., 18g carb. (3g sugars, 1g fiber), 4g pro.

BUTTERBEER

BUTTERBEER

INSPIRED BY: THE WIZARDING WORLD OF HARRY POTTER™ UNIVERSAL ORLANDO RESORT®, *BUTTERBEER*

Witches and wizards, get your Butterbeer here! Bring this fictional drink from the Harry Potter series to life by serving it either foamy and hot in a mug or cold, as shown here.

—Lauren Habermehl, Pewaukee, WI

PREP: 20 min. + chilling
MAKES: 2 servings

BUTTERBEER FOAM
- ¼ cup hot water
- ½ cup marshmallow creme
- ½ envelope whipped topping mix (Dream Whip)
- 1 Tbsp. confectioners' sugar
- 1 pinch salt
- ½ tsp. butterscotch flavoring syrup
- ¼ tsp. butter extract
- ¼ tsp. caramel extract
- ⅛ tsp. vanilla extract

BUTTERBEER
- 2 cans (12 oz. each) cream soda, chilled
- 2 tsp. butterscotch flavoring syrup

1. In a large bowl, stir together the hot water and marshmallow creme until smooth. Freeze for 20-25 minutes or until cool. Stir in whipped topping mix, sugar and salt; blend with a hand mixer until foamy, 30-60 seconds. Stir in the butterscotch syrup and extracts.
2. Pour soda into two 16-oz. mugs; stir in butterscotch syrup. Top with Butterbeer Foam. Serve immediately.

1 serving: 351 cal., 2g fat (2g sat. fat), 0 chol., 138mg sod., 86g carb. (80g sugars, 0 fiber), 0 pro.

BACON PRETZEL FURY

BACON PRETZEL FURY

INSPIRED BY: BUSCH GARDENS®, *BACON PRETZEL FURY*

I tried this treat the last time I was at Busch Gardens, and afterward I ferociously tried to re-create it at home.

—Alvin Ciepluch, Kenosha, WI

PREP: 40 min. + rising
BAKE: 15 min. • **MAKES:** 6 pretzels

- 12 thick-sliced bacon strips
- 1 pkg. (¼ oz.) active dry yeast
- 1½ cups warm water (110° to 115°)
- 2 Tbsp. sugar
- 2 Tbsp. butter, melted
- 1½ tsp. salt
- 4 to 4½ cups all-purpose flour
- ⅓ cup baking soda
- 1 large egg yolk
- 1 Tbsp. cold water
- 1 tsp. coarse salt
- ¼ cup butter, melted
- 6 wooden skewers

1. In a large skillet, cook bacon over medium heat until partially cooked but not crisp. Remove the bacon to paper towels to drain; set aside.
2. In a large bowl, dissolve yeast in warm water. Add sugar, butter, salt and 2 cups flour. Beat until smooth. Stir in enough remaining flour to form a soft dough (dough will be sticky).
3. Turn the dough onto a floured surface; knead for 6-8 minutes until smooth and elastic. Place in a greased bowl, turning once to grease top. Cover and let rise in a warm place until doubled, about 1 hour.
4. Preheat oven to 425°. In a Dutch oven, bring 8 cups water and baking soda to a boil. Punch the dough down; divide into 6 portions. Roll each portion into a 32-in. rope. Fold each rope in half, creating an upside-down V shape. Place 1 bacon strip over the top of each V; braid dough around the bacon, layering in a second bacon strip halfway. Pinch ends to seal; tuck under. Add to the boiling water, 1 at a time; cook 30 seconds. Remove with 2 slotted spoons; drain on paper towels.
5. Place the pretzels on greased baking sheets. Lightly beat egg yolk and cold water; brush over the pretzels. Sprinkle with coarse salt. Bake for 12-15 minutes or until golden brown. Brush with melted butter; sprinkle with additional coarse salt if desired. Remove from the pans to wire racks. Insert skewers; serve warm.

1 pretzel: 533 cal., 21g fat (9g sat. fat), 61mg chol., 1699mg sod., 68g carb. (4g sugars, 3g fiber), 17g pro.

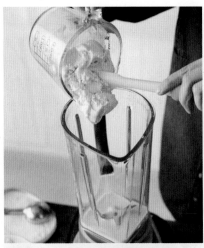

THICK STRAWBERRY SHAKES

HOW-TO

Make the best milkshake ever:
1. **Add the milk, ice cream and mix-ins.** Pour milk in first, and make sure the ice cream is softened.
2. **Blend until smooth.** Keep an eye on the blender so the milkshake is the perfect consistency.
3. **Pour and enjoy!** Pour the milkshake into a chilled glass, then top it off with whipped cream and add all your favorite garnishes.

THICK STRAWBERRY SHAKES

INSPIRED BY: BURGER KING®, *STRAWBERRY SHAKE*

Cool off with a thick and rich treat that will remind you of a malt shoppe!
—*Kathryn Conrad, Milwaukee, WI*

TAKES: 5 min. • **MAKES:** 2 servings

- ⅓ cup 2% milk
- 1½ cups vanilla ice cream
- ½ cup frozen unsweetened strawberries
- 1 Tbsp. strawberry preserves

In a blender, combine all ingredients; cover and process until smooth. Pour into chilled glasses; serve immediately.
1 cup: 257 cal., 12g fat (7g sat. fat), 47mg chol., 100mg sod., 35g carb. (28g sugars, 1g fiber), 5g pro.

DID YOU KNOW?

You should not use heavy cream in shakes in place of milk, even if you need more liquid. The cream would blend into little bits of butter.

COPYCAT CHICK-FIL-A CHICKEN NUGGETS

COPYCAT CHICK-FIL-A CHICKEN NUGGETS
INSPIRED BY: CHICK-FIL-A®,
CHICKEN NUGGETS

I developed this recipe to mimic our favorite restaurant's chicken nuggets. The first time I made them I knew I had a winner: The whole family fought over who got the last one!
—*Jeni Pittard, Statham, GA*

PREP: 20 min. + marinating
COOK: 5 min./batch • **MAKES:** 8 servings

- 2 **lbs. boneless skinless chicken breasts, cut into bite-sized pieces**
- 1 **Tbsp. dill pickle juice**
- ½ **cup cornstarch**
- 1 **Tbsp. soy sauce**
- 1 **large egg white**
- ⅛ **tsp. salt**
- ⅛ **tsp. pepper**
- ¼ **tsp. garlic powder**
- ¼ **tsp. paprika**
- 1 **Tbsp. Dijon mustard**

DIPPING SAUCE
- ¼ **cup Dijon mustard**
- 3 **Tbsp. barbecue sauce**
- 2 **Tbsp. honey**
  Oil for frying

1. Place chicken and pickle juice in a bowl; toss to coat. Let stand at room temperature for 30 minutes. Meanwhile, combine the next 8 ingredients to form a thick batter. Add batter to the chicken mixture and toss to coat.
2. For dipping sauce, combine mustard, barbecue sauce and honey; set aside.
3. In a deep skillet or electric skillet, heat 1 in. oil to 375°. Fry chicken pieces, a few at a time, until browned and juices run clear, 1-2 minutes on each side. Drain on paper towels. Serve with sauce.
1 serving: 307 cal., 16g fat (2g sat. fat), 63mg chol., 514mg sod., 14g carb. (6g sugars, 0 fiber), 24g pro.

HOMEMADE SMILEY FRIES
INSPIRED BY: MCCAIN'S®, *FROZEN SMILEY FRIES*
These cute smiley fries take us back— back to a time with lunch tables, food trays and tiny milk cartons. If you were a hot-lunch kid growing up, there's a strong possibility that you were served smiley fries like these from the cafeteria line on more than one occasion.
—*Lauren Habermehl, Pewaukee, WI*

PREP: 45 min. • **COOK:** 5 min./batch
MAKES: 8 servings

- 2 **cups mashed potatoes (without added milk and butter)**
- ½ **cup dry bread crumbs**
- 2 **Tbsp. cornstarch**
- ½ **tsp. salt**
- ½ **tsp. garlic powder**
- ½ **tsp. onion powder**
- ¼ **tsp. pepper**
  Oil for frying
  Optional: Ketchup, mustard and ranch dressing

1. In a bowl, stir together potatoes, bread crumbs, cornstarch and seasonings until smooth. On a lightly floured surface, roll out the mixture to ¼-in. thickness. Cut with a floured 2-in. round cookie cutter, rerolling scraps. Using a drinking straw, poke 2 circles into each round for eyes. Then use a spoon to make a mouth.
2. In a large skillet or Dutch oven, heat ½ in. oil to 350°. Fry rounds, face-side down, a few at a time, until golden brown, 1-2 minutes on each side. Drain on paper towels; sprinkle with additional salt to taste. Serve warm with optional sauces.
6 fries: 131 cal., 7g fat (1g sat. fat), 0 chol., 208mg sod., 14g carb. (0 sugars, 2g fiber), 2g pro.

**COUNTRY
TURNIP GREENS**

GRANDMA'S CORNBREAD DRESSING
INSPIRED BY: BOSTON MARKET®,
VEGETABLE STUFFING

Growing up, we didn't have turkey. We had chicken, chopped and baked in my grandmother's dressing. Now we leave out the chicken and keep the cornbread dressing.
—Suzanne Mohme, Bastrop, TX

PREP: 40 min. + cooling
BAKE: 45 min. • **MAKES:** 12 servings

- 1   cup all-purpose flour
- 1   cup cornmeal
- 2   tsp. baking powder
- 1   tsp. salt
- 2   large eggs
- 1   cup buttermilk
- ¼   cup canola oil

DRESSING
- 1   Tbsp. canola oil
- 1   medium onion, chopped
- 2   celery ribs, chopped
- 3   large eggs
- 2   cans (10¾ oz. each) condensed cream of chicken soup, undiluted
- 3   tsp. poultry seasoning
- 1   tsp. pepper
- ½   tsp. salt
- 2   cups chicken broth

1. Preheat oven to 400°. In a large bowl, whisk flour, cornmeal, baking powder and salt. In another bowl, whisk eggs and buttermilk. Pour oil into an 8-in. ovenproof skillet; place skillet in oven for 4 minutes.
2. Meanwhile, add buttermilk mixture to flour mixture; stir just until moistened.
3. Carefully tilt and rotate skillet to coat bottom with oil; add batter. Bake until a toothpick inserted in center comes out clean, 20-25 minutes. Cool completely in pan on a wire rack.
4. Reduce oven setting to 350°. For the dressing, in a large skillet, heat the oil over medium-high heat. Add onion and celery; cook and stir 4-6 minutes or until tender. Remove from the heat. Coarsely crumble cornbread into skillet; toss to combine. In a small bowl, whisk eggs, condensed soup and seasonings; stir into bread mixture. Stir in broth.
5. Transfer to a greased 13x9-in. baking dish. Bake for 45-55 minutes or until lightly browned.
⅔ cup: 236 cal., 12g fat (2g sat. fat), 83mg chol., 969mg sod., 25g carb. (2g sugars, 2g fiber), 7g pro.

COUNTRY TURNIP GREENS
INSPIRED BY: CRACKER BARREL®,
TURNIP GREENS

If you've never tried making turnip greens, my recipe is an easy, tasty way to start. Pork and onions give the fresh greens wonderful flavor .
—Sandi Pichon, Memphis, TN

PREP: 10 min. • **COOK:** 45 min.
MAKES: 10 servings

- ¾   lb. lean salt pork or bacon, diced
- 4½ lbs. fresh turnip greens, trimmed
- 1½ cups water
- 1   large onion, chopped
- 1   tsp. sugar
- ¼   to ½ tsp. pepper

1. In a Dutch oven, cook the salt pork until lightly browned. Drain, reserving 2 Tbsp. drippings.
2. Stir the remaining ingredients into the reserved drippings. Bring to a boil. Reduce the heat; cover and simmer for 45 minutes or until greens are tender.
Note: Fresh spinach can be substituted for the turnip greens. Reduce the cooking time to 10 minutes or until the spinach is tender.
½ cup: 317 cal., 28g fat (10g sat. fat), 29mg chol., 622mg sod., 14g carb. (9g sugars, 4g fiber), 4g pro.

WHY YOU'LL LOVE IT...

"I made this for a church party. My hubby loved it, and it made new believers of people who had never tried greens before."
—BEE403, TASTEOFHOME.COM

GRANDMA'S
CORNBREAD
DRESSING

INSPIRED BY
IT'S-IT ICE CREAM®,
ICE CREAM SANDWICH

**ALMOST IT'S-IT
ICE CREAM SANDWICHES,**
P. 110

DOUBLE-TAKE DESSERTS

Don't deprive yourself of all your favorite sweets and treats just because you'd have to drive out to get them. Turn your kitchen into the best ice cream shop or bakery around!

GIRL SCOUT COOKIES

HOMEMADE ICE CREAM SANDWICHES
INSPIRED BY: KLONDIKE BARS®,
KLONDIKE BARS
Why settle for store-bought ice cream sandwiches when you can have ones that taste even better and aren't that difficult to make?
—*Kea Fisher, Bridger, MT*

PREP: 25 min. + freezing
BAKE: 10 min. + cooling
MAKES: 16 servings

- 1   pkg. chocolate cake mix (regular size)
- ¼   cup shortening
- ¼   cup butter, softened
- 1   large egg
- 1   Tbsp. water
- 1   tsp. vanilla extract
- ½   gallon ice cream

1. In a large bowl, combine the cake mix, shortening, butter, egg, water and vanilla until well blended. Divide into 4 equal parts.
2. Between waxed paper, roll 1 part into a 10x6-in. rectangle. Remove top piece of waxed paper and invert dough onto a ungreased baking sheet. Remove the second piece of waxed paper. Score the dough into 8 pieces, each 3x2½ in. Repeat with remaining dough.
3. Bake at 350° for 8-10 minutes or until puffed. Immediately cut along the scored lines and prick holes in each piece with a fork. Cool on wire racks.
4. Cut the ice cream into 16 slices, each 3x2½x1 in. Place an ice cream slice between 2 chocolate cookies; wrap in waxed paper or another wrap. Repeat. Freeze on a baking sheet overnight. May be frozen for up to 2 months.
1 sandwich: 315 cal., 15g fat (8g sat. fat), 48mg chol., 321mg sod., 42g carb. (28g sugars, 1g fiber), 4g pro.

HAVE IT YOUR WAY.
The wonderful thing about ice cream sandwiches? The combinations are almost endless! Some of our favorites include salted caramel ice cream with double chocolate cookies or homemade vanilla ice cream with snickerdoodle cookies, but there are so many other irresistible combinations to discover.

GIRL SCOUT COOKIES
INSPIRED BY: GIRL SCOUT®, *SUGAR COOKIES*
To commemorate the anniversary of the first nationwide sale, the Girl Scouts are pleased to share the original sugar cookie recipe used when the troops made their own cookies.
—*Girl Scout Council*

PREP: 15 min. + chilling
BAKE: 10 min./batch
MAKES: 4 dozen (2½-in. cookies)

- 1   cup butter, softened
- 1   cup sugar
- 2   large eggs, room temperature
- 2   Tbsp. milk
- 1   tsp. vanilla extract
- 2½ cups all-purpose flour
- 2   tsp. baking powder
         Decorator's sugar, optional

1. In a bowl, cream butter and sugar until light and fluffy, 5-7 minutes. Add eggs, 1 at a time, beating well after each addition. Beat in milk and vanilla. Whisk together flour and baking powder; gradually add to the creamed mixture and mix well. Chill for at least 2 hours or overnight.
2. Preheat the oven to 350°. On a lightly floured surface, roll the dough to ¼-in. thickness. Cut with trefoil cookie cutter or cutter of your choice. Place cookies on ungreased baking sheets. Sprinkle with decorator's sugar if desired.
3. Bake for 8-10 minutes or until lightly browned. Cool on wire racks.
Note: This is the original Girl Scout Cookie recipe that was published by the Girl Scout Organization.
1 cookie: 78 cal., 4g fat (3g sat. fat), 18mg chol., 54mg sod., 9g carb. (4g sugars, 0 fiber), 1g pro.

HOMEMADE
ICE CREAM
SANDWICHES

PEPPERMINT BARK

INSPIRED BY: WILLIAMS-SONOMA®,
PEPPERMINT BARK

After sampling peppermint bark from Williams-Sonoma, I thought I could make it myself! Using four ingredients, I came up with a simple version that won over my friends and family.
—*Patti Maurer, Wise, VA*

PREP: 15 min. + chilling
MAKES: 1½ lbs. (24 servings)

- 1 **tsp. plus 3 Tbsp. shortening, divided**
- 1 **pkg. (10 oz.) Andes creme de menthe baking chips**
- 2 **cups white baking chips**
- ½ **cup crushed peppermint candies**

1. Line a 13x9-in. pan with foil; grease foil with 1 tsp. shortening.
2. In a microwave, melt Andes baking chips and 1 Tbsp. shortening; stir until smooth. Pour the mixture into prepared pan. Refrigerate 10 minutes or until set.
3. In top of a double boiler or a metal bowl over barely simmering water, melt baking chips with remaining shortening; stir until smooth. Spread over chocolate layer; sprinkle with crushed candies. Cool. Refrigerate 2 hours or until firm.
4. Break into small pieces. Store in an airtight container.

1 oz.: 161 cal., 10g fat (7g sat. fat), 3mg chol., 19mg sod., 17g carb. (16g sugars, 0 fiber), 1g pro.

MINI PEANUT BUTTER SANDWICH COOKIES

MINI PEANUT BUTTER SANDWICH COOKIES

INSPIRED BY: GIRL SCOUT®, *DO-SI-DOS (AKA PEANUT BUTTER SANDWICH COOKIES)*

Peanut butter lovers go nuts for these little sandwich cookies. To cool down on a hot day, put ice cream between the cookies instead of frosting.
—*Keri Wolfe, Nappanee, IN*

PREP: 25 min.
BAKE: 15 min./batch + cooling
MAKES: about 3½ dozen

- 1 **cup shortening**
- 1 **cup creamy peanut butter**
- 1 **cup sugar**
- 1 **cup packed brown sugar**
- 3 **large eggs, room temperature**
- 1 **tsp. vanilla extract**
- 3½ **cups all-purpose flour**
- 2 **tsp. baking soda**
- ½ **tsp. salt**

FILLING
- ¾ **cup creamy peanut butter**
- ½ **cup 2% milk**
- 1½ **tsp. vanilla extract**
- 4 **cups confectioners' sugar**

1. Preheat oven to 350°. In a large bowl, cream shortening, peanut butter and sugars until blended. Beat in eggs and vanilla. In another bowl, whisk the flour, baking soda and salt; gradually beat into creamed mixture.
2. Shape into 1-in. balls; place 2 in. apart on ungreased baking sheets. Bake until set, 11-13 minutes. Remove from pans to wire racks to cool completely.
3. In a small bowl, beat peanut butter, milk and vanilla until blended. Beat in the confectioners' sugar until smooth. Spread filling on bottoms of half of the cookies; cover with remaining cookies.

Freeze option: Freeze unfilled cookies in freezer containers. To use, thaw cookies and fill as directed.

Note: Reduced-fat peanut butter is not recommended for this recipe.

1 sandwich cookie: 240 cal., 11g fat (2g sat. fat), 14mg chol., 145mg sod., 33g carb. (23g sugars, 1g fiber), 4g pro.

BLACK TIE CHOCOLATE MOUSSE CAKE

BLACK TIE CHOCOLATE MOUSSE CAKE

INSPIRED BY: OLIVE GARDEN®,
BLACK TIE CHOCOLATE MOUSSE CAKE

To slice this cake, run a sharp knife under hot water and dry. Cut the first slice. Rinse the knife under hot water and dry. Repeat with every slice.
—Taste of Home *Test Kitchen*

PREP: 1½ hours + chilling
BAKE: 25 min. + cooling
MAKES: 16 servings

- ½ cup baking cocoa
- 1 cup boiling water
- ½ cup butter, softened
- 1 cup sugar
- 2 large eggs, room temperature
- ¾ tsp. vanilla extract
- 1⅓ cups all-purpose flour
- 1 tsp. baking soda
- ¼ tsp. baking powder
- ¼ tsp. salt

CHOCOLATE CHEESECAKE
- 4 oz. cream cheese, softened
- ¼ cup confectioners' sugar
- ½ tsp. vanilla extract
- ½ cup dark chocolate chips, melted and slightly cooled
- ½ cup heavy whipping cream

WHITE CHOCOLATE MOUSSE
- 1 cup heavy whipping cream
- 2 Tbsp. sugar
- 3 oz. cream cheese, softened
- 3 oz. white baking chocolate, melted and cooled

GANACHE
- 3 cups semisweet chocolate chips
- 1½ cups heavy whipping cream

GARNISH
- 2 cups miniature semisweet chocolate chips
- ¼ cup white baking chips, melted

1. Preheat oven to 350°. In a small bowl, combine cocoa and water; set aside to cool completely. In a large bowl, cream butter and sugar for 5-7 minutes or until light and fluffy. Add the eggs, 1 at a time, beating well after each addition. Beat in the vanilla. Whisk together flour, baking soda, baking powder and salt; add to the creamed mixture alternately with cocoa mixture, beating well after each addition.

2. Pour into a greased, parchment-lined 9-in. round baking pan. Bake until a toothpick inserted in the center comes out clean, 25-30 minutes. Let cool for 10 minutes before removing from pan to a wire rack to cool completely.

3. For chocolate cheesecake layer, in a small bowl, beat the cream cheese, confectioners' sugar and vanilla until smooth. Beat in cooled melted dark chocolate until combined. In another bowl, beat cream until soft peaks form. Fold into cream cheese mixture. Place cake layer in bottom of a 9-in. springform pan; spread the cheesecake over top. Refrigerate until chilled, about 1 hour.

4. For white chocolate mousse, in a bowl beat the cream until it begins to thicken. Gradually add sugar, beating until stiff peaks form; set aside. In another bowl, beat cream cheese until fluffy. Add white chocolate and beat until smooth. Fold in whipped cream. Spread over chocolate cheesecake layer. Refrigerate until set and chilled, about 1 hour.

5. For ganache, place chips in a large bowl. In a small saucepan, bring cream just to a boil. Pour over chocolate; stir with a whisk until smooth.

6. Cool slightly, stirring occasionally. Reserve ¾ cup for frosting; cover and refrigerate until cold.

7. Remove cake from pan; place on a wire rack. Pour remaining ganache over cake, allowing it to coat sides. For garnish, press the miniature chocolate chips into sides of cake. Drizzle melted white chips over the top. Refrigerate, covered, until chilled. Beat reserved ganache until piping consistency, about 15 seconds. Pipe around top edges. Refrigerate until serving.

1 piece: 696 cal., 48g fat (29g sat. fat), 102mg chol., 241mg sod., 71g carb. (56g sugars, 4g fiber), 8g pro.

COPYCAT NOTHING
BUNDT CAKE

COPYCAT NOTHING BUNDT CAKE

INSPIRED BY: NOTHING BUNDT CAKES®, *CHOCOLATE CHOCOLATE CHIP CAKE*

My kids love chocolate, so I'm always looking for a way to kick it up a little. This recipe is moist, delicious and so easy to make.
—*Elizabeth Wynne, Aztec, NM*

PREP: 15 min. • **COOK:** 40 min.
MAKES: 16 servings

- 1 pkg. devil's food cake mix (regular size)
- 1 pkg. (3.9 oz.) instant chocolate pudding mix
- 1 cup sour cream
- ½ cup canola oil
- ½ cup water
- 4 large eggs, room temperature
- 3 tsp. vanilla extract
- 1 cup semisweet chocolate chips

FROSTING
- 1 pkg. (8 oz.) cream cheese, softened
- ¼ cup butter, softened
- 1½ tsp. vanilla extract
- 3 cups confectioners' sugar

1. Preheat the oven to 350°. Grease and flour a 10-in. fluted tube pan.
2. In a bowl, combine first 7 ingredients; beat on low speed for 30 seconds. Beat on medium 2 minutes. Stir in chocolate chips. Transfer to prepared pan. Bake until a toothpick inserted near the center comes out clean, 35-40 minutes. Cool in pan 10 minutes before removing to a wire rack to cool completely.
3. In a bowl, beat cream cheese, butter and vanilla until smooth. Gradually beat in confectioners' sugar. Pipe or spread over top of cake.

1 piece: 460 cal., 23g fat (10g sat. fat), 79mg chol., 370mg sod., 61g carb. (44g sugars, 1g fiber), 5g pro.

COPY THAT!

When you flip the tube pan over, the cake should slip out, especially if you greased the pan properly and waited for the cake to cool. If it doesn't budge, lay a dish towel over the counter, turn the pan upside down and tap the base. If it still doesn't budge, leave it there for a while. Eventually gravity should do the trick.

HOMEMADE OREO COOKIES

HOMEMADE OREO COOKIES

INSPIRED BY: OREO®, *OREO COOKIES*

An embossing pin, if you have it, lets you quickly make cookies with a raised design. If you don't have one, thin the cookie dough with hot coffee to a pipeable consistency and create your own designs.
—*Christine Rukavena, Milwaukee, WI*

PREP: 40 min. + chilling
BAKE: 10 min./batch + cooling
MAKES: 3 dozen

- ¾ cup unsalted butter, softened
- 1 cup sugar
- ⅓ cup packed brown sugar
- 1 large egg, room temperature
- 1 large egg yolk, room temperature
- 1¼ tsp. vanilla extract
- 1⅔ cups all-purpose flour
- 1 cup baking cocoa
- ½ tsp. salt
- ½ tsp. baking powder
- 2 to 3 tsp. hot brewed coffee, optional

FILLING
- ⅓ cup shortening
- ⅓ cup unsalted butter, softened
- 1¼ tsp. vanilla extract
- 2¼ cups confectioners' sugar
- ⅓ cup marshmallow creme

1. In a mixing bowl, cream butter and sugars until light and fluffy, 5-7 minutes. Beat in egg, yolk and vanilla. Sift together the flour, cocoa, salt and baking powder. Gradually add to the creamed mixture.

2. Divide the dough in half; roll each between sheets of floured parchment into 8-in. disks. Refrigerate 30 minutes or until firm enough to roll.
3. Preheat oven to 325°. Roll each portion of dough directly on parchment-lined baking sheets to ⅛-in. thickness.
4. If using an embossing pin, brush the embossing pin with cocoa to prevent sticking; roll the pin over dough to transfer design.
5. Cut the dough with a floured 2-in. round cookie cutter, leaving at least ½ in. between cookies. Remove trimmings. (If dough becomes too soft, chill as needed.)
6. If desired, combine 3 Tbsp. dough and enough hot coffee to reach piping consistency; transfer thinned dough to a pastry bag fitted with a #1 round tip. Decorate cutouts as desired.
7. Bake for 10-12 minutes or until firm. Cool on pans 2 minutes. Remove to wire racks to cool completely.
8. For filling, beat shortening, butter and vanilla until blended. Gradually beat in confectioners' sugar and marshmallow creme until smooth. Spread filling on bottoms of half the cookies; cover with remaining cookies. Store cookies in an airtight container.

1 sandwich cookie: 159 cal., 8g fat (4g sat. fat), 25mg chol., 44mg sod., 22g carb. (16g sugars, 1g fiber), 1g pro.

COPYCAT CELEBRATION CHEESECAKE

INSPIRED BY: CHEESECAKE FACTORY®, *CELEBRATION CHEESECAKE*

Both of my children were born on the same day but five years apart, so I like to make an elaborate dessert to celebrate both of their birthdays. This seven-layered beauty really fits the bill. The baking and preparation are easy, but do set aside some time for assembly. Everyone will be amazed when they see the final product.
—*Kristyne McDougle Walter, Lorain, OH*

PREP: 1 hour + freezing
BAKE: 30 min. + cooling
MAKES: 16 servings

- 4 cups cold 2% milk
- 3 pkg. (3.4 oz. each) instant white chocolate pudding mix
- 1 pkg. white cake mix (regular size)
- 1⅓ cups rainbow sprinkles, divided
- 1 pkg. (1 oz.) freeze-dried strawberries
- 3 to 12 drops blue food coloring
- ¼ cup baking cocoa
- 2 cartons (24.3 oz. each) Philadelphia ready-to-serve cheesecake filling
- 2 cans (16 oz. each) cream cheese frosting
- 2 Tbsp. rainbow sequin sprinkles

1. Preheat the oven to 350°. In each of 3 small bowls, whisk 1⅓ cups milk and 1 pkg. pudding mix for 2 minutes. Refrigerate, covered, while baking the cake layers.
2. Line bottoms of 2 greased 9-in. round baking pans with parchment; grease the paper. Prepare the cake mix batter according to package directions, folding ⅔ cup sprinkles into batter. Transfer to prepared pans. Bake and cool as the package directs.
3. Using a long serrated knife, trim tops of the cake layers to level. Crumble trimmings; transfer to a parchment-lined baking sheet. Bake at 350° until crisp but not browned, about 5 minutes. Cool completely on pan on wire rack.
4. Line two 9-in. springform pans with plastic, letting ends extend over sides. Place strawberries in a food processor; process until ground. Stir strawberries into 1 bowl of pudding. To another bowl of pudding, whisk in blue food coloring. To the third bowl, whisk in the cocoa; refrigerate chocolate pudding.

5. Place 1 cake layer in 1 prepared springform pan; spread with strawberry pudding. Place remaining cake layer in remaining prepared springform pan; spread with blue pudding. Freeze both pans for at least 1 hour. Top each with 1 carton cheesecake filling. Freeze at least 1 hour longer.
6. Remove strawberry-layered pan from freezer; spread chocolate pudding over top. Return to the freezer for 3 hours. Meanwhile, stir the remaining ⅔ cup sprinkles into cooled cake crumbs.
7. Remove rims from springform pans; discard plastic. Place the strawberry-layered cake on a serving plate; top with the blue-layered cake. Frost top and sides with cream cheese frosting. Gently press crumb mixture into frosting on sides of cake; sprinkle with sequins. Freeze until ready to serve. Remove 10 minutes before cutting.

1 piece: 871 cal., 43g fat (19g sat. fat), 120mg chol., 929mg sod., 114g carb. (90g sugars, 1g fiber), 9g pro.

COPYCAT CELEBRATION CHEESECAKE

COPY THAT!

Don't be tempted to skip the freezing of the pudding layers before adding the cheesecake layer on top. Doing so allows the pudding layers to better set and results in crisp, cleanly delineated layers.

CALIFORNIA PIZZA KITCHEN BUTTER CAKE

THE FAMOUS DOUBLETREE COOKIE
INSPIRED BY: DOUBLETREE®,
CHOCOLATE CHIP COOKIES
We tested this recipe for family and friends, following every last step right down to the fussiest detail—including letting the cookies cool for an hour.
—Taste of Home *Test Kitchen*

PREP: 25 min.
BAKE: 20 min./batch + cooling
MAKES: about 2½ dozen

- 1 cup butter, softened
- ¾ cup plus 1 Tbsp. sugar
- ¾ cup packed brown sugar
- 2 large eggs, room temperature
- 1¼ tsp. vanilla extract
- ¼ tsp. lemon juice
- 2¼ cups all-purpose flour
- ½ cup old-fashioned oats
- 1 tsp. baking soda
- 1 tsp. salt
  Dash ground cinnamon
- 2⅔ cups semisweet chocolate chips
- 1¾ cups chopped walnuts

1. Preheat the oven to 300°. Cream the butter and sugars until light and fluffy, 5-7 minutes. Beat in eggs, vanilla and lemon juice. Whisk together flour, oats, baking soda, salt and cinnamon. Fold into creamed mixture with chocolate chips and walnuts.
2. Drop dough by 3 tablespoonfuls 2 in. apart onto parchment-lined baking sheets. Bake until edges begin to brown and center is soft, 20-23 minutes. Cool on pans 1 hour until fully cooled and set.
1 cookie: 241 cal., 15g fat (7g sat. fat), 27mg chol., 167mg sod., 28g carb. (18g sugars, 2g fiber), 3g pro.

CALIFORNIA PIZZA KITCHEN BUTTER CAKE
INSPIRED BY: CALIFORNIA PIZZA KITCHEN®,
BUTTER CAKE
I love dining at California Pizza Kitchen and was wondering if there was a way to get my hands on the butter cake recipe—it's to die for! After a couple of attempts, I think I got the recipe just about perfect.
—*Madeeha Anwar, Woodbridge, VA*

PREP: 25 min. • **BAKE:** 35 min.
MAKES: 8 servings

- 1 Tbsp. plus 1 cup sugar
- 1 cup butter, room temperature
- 1 tsp. vanilla extract
- 1 tsp. almond extract
- 3 large eggs, room temperature
- 1½ cups all-purpose flour
- 1 tsp. baking powder
- 1 cup buttermilk, room temperature
  Vanilla ice cream, optional

1. Preheat oven to 375°. Line bottom of a greased 9-in. round baking pan with parchment; grease paper. Dust bottom and sides with 1 Tbsp. sugar.
2. In a large bowl, beat butter, remaining 1 cup sugar and extracts until light and fluffy, 5-7 minutes. Add the eggs, 1 at a time, beating well after each addition. In another bowl, whisk flour and baking powder; add to the creamed mixture alternately with buttermilk, beating well after each addition.
3. Transfer to prepared pan. Bake until a toothpick inserted in the center comes out clean, 35-40 minutes. Cool 5 minutes before transferring to a wire rack to cool completely. If desired, serve cake with ice cream.
1 piece: 319 cal., 25g fat (15g sat. fat), 131mg chol., 210mg sod., 18g carb. (0 sugars, 1g fiber), 5g pro.

CREAM-FILLED CUPCAKES

BOURBON & CORNFLAKES ICE CREAM

INSPIRED BY: HUMPHRY SLOCOMBE®, *SECRET BREAKFAST ICE CREAM*

Humphry Slocombe's Secret Breakfast is a vanilla-based ice cream infused with bourbon and cornflake cookies. I came up with this recipe for friends who aren't able to find Humphry Slocombes.
—*Andrea Potischman, Menlo Park, CA*

PREP: 45 min. + chilling
PROCESS: 30 min. + freezing
MAKES: 1 qt.

- 3 Tbsp. heavy whipping cream
- 3 Tbsp. unsalted butter, melted
- 2 Tbsp. sugar
  Dash salt
- 1½ cups cornflakes, coarsely crushed

VANILLA BOURBON ICE CREAM
- 5 large egg yolks
- ½ cup sugar
  Dash salt
- 1 cup whole milk
- 1½ cups heavy whipping cream
- 1 tsp. vanilla extract
- 3 Tbsp. bourbon

1. Preheat oven to 375°. In a small bowl, combine cream, butter, sugar and salt. Stir in the cornflakes until well coated. Spread onto a parchment-lined baking sheet. Bake 12-15 minutes or until golden brown, stirring once. Cool completely.
2. For the ice cream, in a large heavy saucepan, whisk the egg yolks, sugar and salt until blended; stir in the milk. Cook over low heat until the mixture is just thick enough to coat a metal spoon and a thermometer reads at least 160°, stirring constantly. Do not allow to boil. Remove from heat immediately.
3. Quickly transfer to a small bowl; place bowl in a pan of ice water. Stir gently and occasionally for 2 minutes. Stir in cream and vanilla. Press the waxed paper onto surface of custard. Refrigerate several hours or overnight.
4. Stir bourbon into the custard. Fill cylinder of an ice cream maker no more than two-thirds full; freeze according to manufacturer's directions, adding cornflakes during the last 2 minutes of processing. (Refrigerate any remaining mixture until ready to freeze.)
5. Transfer the ice cream to freezer containers, allowing headspace for expansion. Freeze until firm, 2-4 hours.
½ cup: 353 cal., 26g fat (16g sat. fat), 187mg chol., 108mg sod., 23g carb. (19g sugars, 0 fiber), 5g pro.

CREAM-FILLED CUPCAKES

INSPIRED BY: HOSTESS®, *CUPCAKES*

These chocolate cupcakes have a fun filling and shiny chocolate frosting that make them extra special. They always disappear in a flash!
—*Kathy Kittell, Lenexa, KS*

PREP: 20 min.
BAKE: 15 min. + cooling
MAKES: 2 dozen

- 1 pkg. devil's food cake mix (regular size)
- 2 tsp. hot water
- ¼ tsp. salt
- 1 jar (7 oz.) marshmallow creme
- ½ cup shortening
- ⅓ cup confectioners' sugar
- ½ tsp. vanilla extract

GANACHE FROSTING
- 1 cup semisweet chocolate chips
- ¾ cup heavy whipping cream

1. Prepare and bake the cake batter according to the package directions, using 24 paper-lined muffin cups. Cool 5 minutes before removing from pans to wire racks to cool completely.
2. For filling, in a small bowl, combine the water and salt until salt is dissolved. Cool. In a small bowl, beat marshmallow creme, shortening, confectioners' sugar and vanilla until light and fluffy; beat in the salt mixture.
3. Transfer cream filling to a pastry bag fitted with a round pastry tip. Push tip through the top of each cupcake to fill center.
4. Place chocolate chips in a small bowl. In a small saucepan, bring cream just to a boil. Pour over chocolate; whisk until smooth. Cool, stirring occasionally, to room temperature or until the ganache reaches a dipping consistency.
5. Dip cupcake tops in ganache; chill for 20 minutes or until set. Store in the refrigerator.
1 cupcake: 262 cal., 15g fat (5g sat. fat), 32mg chol., 223mg sod., 29g carb. (20g sugars, 1g fiber), 2g pro.

WHY YOU'LL LOVE IT ...

"If you love chocolate, then this is the recipe for you. It's easy to make and delicious!"
—SMDOUG, TASTEOFHOME.COM

BOURBON &
CORNFLAKES
ICE CREAM

COPYCAT CHEESECAKE FACTORY ORIGINAL CHEESECAKE

HOW-TO

Plate like a Pro

A hot knife is the secret to cutting tidy slices of cake and cheesecake. You'll need a sharp knife, some hot water and a towel. Dip the blade into water to heat, then wipe dry and cut. Repeat each time for pretty slices with clean edges.

COPYCAT CHEESECAKE FACTORY ORIGINAL CHEESECAKE

INSPIRED BY: CHEESECAKE FACTORY®, *ORIGINAL CHEESECAKE*

If you're going to prepare cheesecake, why not re-create one of the most popular desserts in the country? It's easier than you think when you follow this four-step recipe.
—Taste of Home *Test Kitchen*

PREP: 30 min. + cooling
BAKE: 1½ hours + chilling
MAKES: 16 servings

- 2½ **cups graham cracker crumbs**
- ¼ **cup sugar**
- ½ **cup butter, melted**

FILLING
- 4 **pkg. (8 oz. each) cream cheese, softened**
- 2 **cups sour cream**
- 1¾ **cups sugar**
- 1 **Tbsp. vanilla extract**
- 4 **large eggs, room temperature, lightly beaten**

TOPPING
- 1 **cup sour cream**
- ¼ **cup sugar**

1. Preheat oven to 325°. In a small bowl, combine graham cracker crumbs and sugar; stir in the butter. Press onto the bottom and up the sides of a greased 9-in. springform pan. Place on a baking sheet. Bake 18-22 minutes until lightly browned. Cool on a wire rack.

2. In a large bowl, beat cream cheese, sour cream, sugar and vanilla until smooth. Add eggs; beat on low speed just until combined. Pour into crust. Place pan on a double thickness of heavy-duty foil (about 18 in. square). Securely wrap foil around pan.

3. Place in a larger baking pan; add 1 in. hot water to larger pan. Bake until center is just set and top appears dull, about 1½ hours. Remove springform pan from the water bath. Let stand for 5 minutes on a wire rack.

4. For topping, in a small bowl, mix sour cream and sugar; spread over the top of cheesecake. Bake 5 minutes longer without water bath. Cool 10 minutes on wire rack. Loosen sides from pan with a knife; remove foil. Cool 1 hour longer. Refrigerate overnight, covering when completely cooled. Remove rim from pan.

1 piece: 536 cal., 37g fat (21g sat. fat), 151mg chol., 329mg sod., 45g carb. (36g sugars, 1g fiber), 8g pro.

**CONTEST-WINNING
MOIST CHOCOLATE CAKE**

FRESH FRUIT COBBLER
INSPIRED BY: CRACKER BARREL®,
FRUIT COBBLER

I received this recipe years ago. It's a family favorite, especially when Maine blueberries are in season. What a treat to eat on a hot summer day!
—*Paula Chick, Lewiston, ME*

PREP: 15 min. • **BAKE:** 40 min.
MAKES: 12 servings

CONTEST-WINNING MOIST CHOCOLATE CAKE
INSPIRED BY: KFC®, *CHOCOLATE CHIP CAKE*
You don't have to spend a lot of time to serve an elegant and delicious dessert. You can quickly mix up the batter in one bowl, bake the cake and serve a crowd.
—*Christa Hageman, Telford, PA*

PREP: 15 min.
BAKE: 45 min. + cooling
MAKES: 12 servings

- 2 cups sugar
- 1¾ cups all-purpose flour
- ¾ cup baking cocoa
- 2 tsp. baking soda
- 1 tsp. baking powder
- 1 tsp. salt
- 2 large eggs
- 1 cup strong brewed coffee, cooled
- 1 cup buttermilk
- ½ cup canola oil
- 1 tsp. vanilla extract
- 1 Tbsp. confectioners' sugar

1. In a large bowl, combine the first 6 ingredients. Add the eggs, coffee, buttermilk, oil and vanilla; beat on medium speed for 2 minutes (batter will be thin). Pour into a greased and floured 10-in. fluted tube pan.
2. Bake at 350° for 45-50 minutes or until a toothpick inserted in the center comes out clean. Cool for 10 minutes before removing from pan to a wire rack to cool completely. Dust with confectioners' sugar.
Note: To substitute for each cup of buttermilk, use 1 Tbsp. white vinegar or lemon juice plus enough milk to measure 1 cup. Stir, then let stand for 5 minutes. Or, use 1 cup plain yogurt or 1¾ tsp. cream of tartar plus 1 cup milk.
1 slice: 315 cal., 11g fat (2g sat. fat), 36mg chol., 473mg sod., 52g carb. (34g sugars, 1g fiber), 5g pro.

WHY YOU'LL LOVE IT ...
"Very moist! Not a crumb is left after I serve it to my family. It is the most-requested cake from my husband!"
—JESICA, TASTEOFHOME.COM

- 5 to 6 cups chopped fresh fruit (apples, rhubarb, blueberries or peaches)
- 2 cups all-purpose flour
- ½ cup sugar
- 4 tsp. baking powder
- 1 tsp. salt
- ½ cup cold butter, cubed
- 1 cup 2% milk
TOPPING
- ⅔ cup sugar
- ¼ cup cornstarch
- 1½ cups boiling water

1. Preheat oven to 350°. Arrange the fruit evenly in the bottom of a 13x9-in. greased baking dish.
2. In a bowl, combine the flour, sugar, baking powder and salt; cut in butter until crumbly. Stir in milk. Spoon over fruit. Combine sugar and cornstarch; sprinkle over batter. Pour water over all. Bake until fruit is tender and topping is golden, 40-45 minutes.
1 serving: 267 cal., 8g fat (5g sat. fat), 22mg chol., 428mg sod., 46g carb. (26g sugars, 2g fiber), 3g pro.

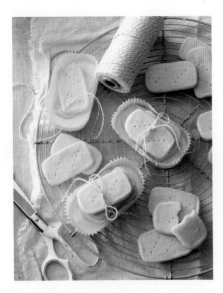

ALMOST IT'S-IT ICE CREAM SANDWICHES

SHORTBREAD

INSPIRED BY: GIRL SCOUT®, *SHORTBREAD (AKA GIRL SCOUT TREFOILS)*

I reside in Missouri now, but many family recipes come from New Zealand, where I lived as a youngster. I proudly lay claim to a Down Under heritage! These special-occasion cookies bring back warm and sweet memories of my childhood, and I'm going to make sure they're passed on to the next generation in my family, no matter where they live!

—A. Swenson, Camdenton, MO

PREP: 15 min. + chilling
BAKE: 10 min./batch
MAKES: 5 dozen

- 1 cup butter, softened
- ½ cup sugar
- ½ cup confectioners' sugar
- 2 cups all-purpose flour
- ½ cup cornstarch
- ½ tsp. salt

1. In large bowl, cream the butter and sugars until light and fluffy, 5-7 minutes. Combine the flour, cornstarch and salt; gradually add to creamed mixture and mix well. Roll dough into a 15x2x1-in. rectangle; chill.
2. Preheat oven to 325°. Cut into ¼-in. slices; place 2 in. apart on ungreased baking sheets. Prick with a fork. Bake 10-12 minutes or until set. Remove to wire racks to cool.

1 cookie: 57 cal., 3g fat (2g sat. fat), 8mg chol., 44mg sod., 7g carb. (3g sugars, 0 fiber), 0 pro.

ALMOST IT'S-IT ICE CREAM SANDWICHES

INSPIRED BY: IT'S-IT ICE CREAM®, *ICE CREAM SANDWICH*

You'll discover why this treat is so popular in San Francisco. It's like snack heaven—ice cream, oatmeal cookies and a touch of chocolate. Replace the vanilla ice cream with your favorite flavor, such as chocolate, caramel or cherry.

—Jacyn Siebert, San Francisco, CA

PREP: 40 min. + freezing
BAKE: 15 min./batch + cooling
MAKES: 7 servings

- ½ cup butter, softened
- ¾ cup packed brown sugar
- ¼ cup sugar
- 1 large egg, room temperature
- ½ tsp. vanilla extract
- ¾ cup all-purpose flour
- ½ tsp. baking soda
- ½ tsp. ground cinnamon
- ¼ tsp. baking powder
- ¼ tsp. salt
- 1½ cups quick-cooking oats
- ¼ cup chopped raisins, optional

ASSEMBLY

- 3 cups vanilla ice cream
- 1 bottle (7¼ oz.) chocolate hard-shell ice cream topping
  Optional: Sprinkles, chopped nuts and miniature semisweet chocolate chips

1. Preheat oven to 350°. In a large bowl, cream butter and sugars until light and fluffy, 5-7 minutes. Beat in the egg and vanilla. In another bowl, whisk flour, baking soda, cinnamon, baking powder and salt; gradually beat into creamed mixture. Stir in oats and, if desired, chopped raisins.
2. Shape into fourteen 1¼-in. balls; place 2½ in. apart on ungreased baking sheets. Bake 11-13 minutes or until golden brown. Cool on pans 3 minutes. Remove to wire racks to cool completely.
3. To assemble ice cream sandwiches, place ⅓ cup ice cream on bottom of a cookie. Top with a second cookie, pressing gently to flatten ice cream; place on a baking sheet. Repeat with remaining cookies and ice cream. Freeze until firm.
4. Remove ice cream sandwiches from the freezer. Working over a small bowl, drizzle chocolate topping over half of each sandwich, allowing the excess to drip off. If desired, roll the other edge in sprinkles, nuts or chocolate chips.
5. Place on a waxed paper-lined baking sheet; freeze until serving. For longer storage, wrap individually in waxed paper and place in a sealed freezer container.

1 ice cream sandwich: 580 cal., 29g fat (16g sat. fat), 86mg chol., 364mg sod., 74g carb. (50g sugars, 3g fiber), 7g pro.

RECIPE INDEX